501 Quilting Motifs

DESIGNS FOR HAND OR MACHINE QUILTING

FROM THE EDITORS OF

Quiltmaker
The Quilts You Want to Make—We Show You How

MAGAZINE

Martingale
Create with Confidence

501 Quilting Motifs:
Designs for Hand or Machine Quilting
© 2011 from the Editors of *Quiltmaker* Magazine

Martingale®
19021 120th Ave. NE, Suite 102
Bothell, WA 98011-9511 USA
ShopMartingale.com

Credits

President & CEO: Tom Wierzbicki
Editor in Chief: Mary V. Green
Managing Editor: Tina Cook
Developmental Editor: Karen Costello Soltys
Copy Editor: Marcy Heffernan
Design Director: Stan Green
Production Manager: Regina Girard
Illustrator: Laurel Strand
Cover & Text Designer: Stan Green

Mission Statement

Dedicated to providing quality products
and service to inspire creativity.

The information in this book is presented in good faith; however, no warranty is given nor are results guaranteed. *Quiltmaker,* Martingale, and Creative Crafts Group, LLC, disclaim any and all liability for untoward results.

Quiltmaker, ISSN 1047-1634, is published bimonthly by Creative Crafts Group, LLC, 741 Corporate Circle, Suite A, Golden, CO 80401, www.quiltmaker.com.

Printed in China
19 18 17 16 15 14   8 7 6 5 4 3 2 1

Library of Congress Cataloging-in-Publication Data is available upon request.

ISBN: 978-1-60468-438-4

 This Symbol Means the Design Is Digitized for Quilting

Many of the designs in *Quiltmaker's* extensive library of motifs are available for use on computer-guided quilting machines. Visit quiltmaker.com to purchase. Formats available include Statler Stitcher, CompuQuilter, and IntelliQuilter.

Table of Contents

Welcome

Welcome to *501 Quilting Motifs: Designs for Hand or Machine Quilting*. This book includes beautiful quilting motifs to enhance patchwork or appliqué. You'll find a variety of styles and sizes. Variations on each motif provide alternatives for your projects. We include an extensive index that allows you to search for a motif alphabetically or by size. We hope you find this collection an inspiring resource as you create the rich surface textures of your quilt.

How to Use This Book

Please note that the measurements for the quilt blocks and borders are *finished* sizes into which the motifs can fit. Seam allowances are already hidden by the time you get to the quilting step.

To find a motif to fit a specific space, refer to the "Size Index" on page 202 for suggestions. When you need quilting inspiration, just leaf through the pages.

Selecting Motifs

Answering these questions will help narrow down motif possibilities.

What is the style of my quilt? For a formal, traditional quilt, look for circular motifs, feathers, or flowers. You can enhance the formal style of your quilt by centering motifs on each plain block.

If you're leaning toward an informal, casual look, less-defined shapes work well. You may want to position motifs randomly or use a combination of motifs in different areas to enhance the style.

Do I want to enhance or contrast the lines of the quilt top? If your quilt is made up of diagonals that you want to enhance, choose an angular, geometric motif. If you want to soften the appearance of the diagonal lines, choose a gentler and more rounded motif.

What size space do I need to fill? The "Size Index" will help you find a motif to fit the space to be quilted. If the motif you choose doesn't have an option that fits, see "Adapting Motifs" on page 4.

Does the space I need to fill have a busy print or a plain print? Solid-colored fabric is the perfect place to showcase an intricate quilting motif you love. The same motif on a busy print will get lost, and your quilting will go unnoticed.

Am I machine quilting or hand quilting?
Hand quilting allows most any kind of design without limitations. Make sure you find a motif that will showcase all the time you put into the quilting. If machine quilting is your method of choice, you may want to focus on continuous-line patterns. You can complete individual motifs without having to start and stop sewing. If you select a motif that's not a continuous-line pattern, keep in mind that you'll have to begin and end the line wherever it dead-ends. Adapt the motif to make it continuous. Make sure to start and stop any lines of quilting with tiny stitches to anchor them.

How accomplished am I as a quilter? If the thought of quilting even one of those detailed motifs strikes fear in your heart, choosing one for your queen-size quilt project will only mean that the quilt never gets done. Choose something simpler that you will be happy with, saving the detailed motif for a pillow top that requires only one design. If you love to quilt and can't wait to tackle the biggies, go for it!

How much quilting do I need? As with many quilting questions, the answer is "it depends." It depends on the look you're trying to achieve, the batting you use, and how the quilt will be used. In general, plan for a consistent density across your quilt. Expand your vision beyond the border and block seams. Quilt across all the borders or bring a block motif into empty spaces along a border motif. Read your batting manufacturer's instructions to know the minimum amount of quilting required. If you're making a quilt that will be washed frequently, give it the security of a lot of quilting. If you're making a wall quilt, you can get away with less quilting if that's the look you want.

Adapting Motifs

You've found a motif you love, but it isn't exactly what you need. Here are some ways to adapt the motif you can't live without.

Change the Size
The easiest way to adjust the size of a motif is with a photocopy machine. First, make a paper shape that represents the space for the motif. Then reduce or enlarge the motif on the copier until it fits into the paper shape. Layering the two papers and holding them up to a light is a good way to check.

Consider an Alternative Placement
Who says a motif has to fit inside a block? If your motif is too large, perhaps it can break the boundaries of the block and overlap into other areas of the quilt. If it fits the style of the quilt, why not?

Consider Filling in the Space with Other Quilting
If your motif is small and you don't want multiple shapes but need more quilting, use another method such as those shown below to fill in the space.

For a formal look, add a grid behind the motif.

Machine stipple around the motif to cover areas quickly and make the motif stand out.

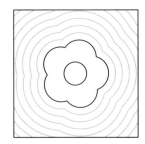

Echo quilt around the motif to emphasize the shape of the central design.

Make a Motif Continuous
If the motif has more starts and stops than you want to quilt, you can always add more quilting lines.

Add lines for a continuous motif.

Quilt Continuously Between Motifs

Quilt a complementary line to travel from one motif to the next, echo a portion of the motif, or quilt in a seam line to move to the next motif. Consider adding tendrils or curls to fill spaces between motifs.

Add lines and shapes to fill spaces.

Transferring Motifs

Mark your quilt before layering and basting. The most common way to transfer a design is to trace the quilting motif onto tracing paper. Place the tracing paper under the quilt top with a light source under it. A portable light box works well. Lightly mark the design on the quilt top with the marking tool of your choice. Refer to "Marking Tools" on page 6 for marking options.

If your quilt fabrics are dark, you may prefer to trace around a template rather than use a light box. To make a template, trace the motif on heavy clear plastic using a permanent marker. If the design is closed, simply cut on the marked outer line. For a more intricate motif, use a craft knife to cut out the lines, cutting a wide enough channel to accommodate your marking tool. You can also buy a double-bladed knife made specifically for cutting channels.

Positioning Motifs and Variations

Refer to the instructions below for help with positioning motifs on your block or patch.

Finding the Center

For a centered motif, find the center of the block by folding the fabric in half lengthwise, and then crosswise, and lightly finger-pressing. When unfolded, the creases will help you center the motif for tracing.

Finding Diagonal Lines

Many variations are lined up with diagonal lines. To position these, cut a piece of tracing paper to the size of the finished block. Fold in half from corner to corner, and then fold in half again. Lightly finger-press. When unfolded, the creases can be used to line up motifs to create the whole design.

Eight-Point Circles

Some design options rely on circles for motif placement. You will find ¼-circle patterns on page 201. The patterns include all the circle sizes used in this book. To draw a circular motif, first find the center of your tracing paper by folding. Next, open up the paper, align the center marks, and trace the arc. Then, rotating the paper ¼ turn each time, repeat the tracing to make a complete circle.

For example, an 11½" block for the "Rosebush" motif on page 65 has leaves spaced around a circle. To draw this design, place a dot where each fold crosses the circle. Line up the motifs on the dots, trace, and repeat until the circle is complete.

Finding Vertical, Horizontal, and Diagonal Lines

For some designs, you'll need guidelines in several directions. Fold the paper lengthwise and crosswise; then open it out and refold it corner to corner to get horizontal, vertical, and diagonal lines.

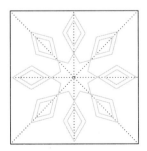

Six-Point Circles

To position some designs, use a combination of the circle and angle patterns on page 201. For example, a variation for the Ivy 1 motif on page 180 uses only three repeats. To draw this design, draw a 4" circle, and then draw lines at 60° angles, as shown. Place three dots on the circle, one at every other intersection of the lines and the circle. Starting at each dot, trace the motif three times. In this case, the circle becomes part of the quilting design. Be sure to trace it when transferring the design to the quilt top.

Marking Tools

Every quilter, for one reason or another, will have her favorite way of marking a quilt. This table helps you identify tools to find your own preferences. Test any marking product for removability before using it on your quilt.

Product	Description	Type of Quilting	Advantages	Concerns	Template Required
Pencil	Quilter's colored pencils, mechanical pencils	Hand	Thin line usually disappears under stitching, easily erased	Often not dark enough to be seen for machine quilting	Yes
Chalk	Tailor's chalk, chalk dispensers, chalk pencils	Hand/machine	Comes in a variety of colors, erases easily with rubbing	Can rub off before you want it to	Yes
Soap	Soapstone, soap slivers	Hand	Easily washed out, economical, shows well on dark fabrics	Often not dark enough to be seen on light fabrics and prints	Yes
Markers	Air-erase markers, washable markers	Hand/machine	Good dark line	Some quilters worry about marks reappearing	Yes
Hera marker	Tool that creases the quilt to show markings	Hand/machine	Makes no permanent mark	Can be difficult to see, can wear off before you want it to	Yes
Tape	Masking tape, narrow tape with marked lines	Hand/machine	Peels off easily, marking of quilt top not necessary, can be reused	Only for straight lines or very gentle curves	No
Quilter's guide on machine	Bar attaches to the walking foot on some machines	Machine	Marking of quilt top not necessary	Best for straight lines with a guide to follow	No
Tracing paper	Motif is traced on paper and pinned to quilt top	Machine	Marking of quilt top not necessary	Motif must be traced on every sheet	No

Children/Teens

Dolphin Bay

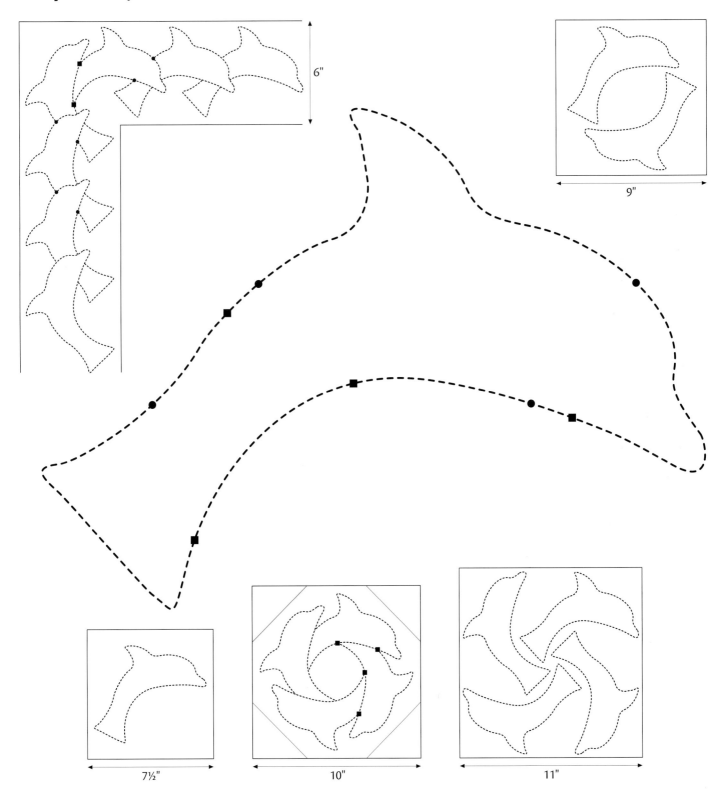

6"

9"

7½"

10"

11"

☺ 7

Floating Clouds and Stars

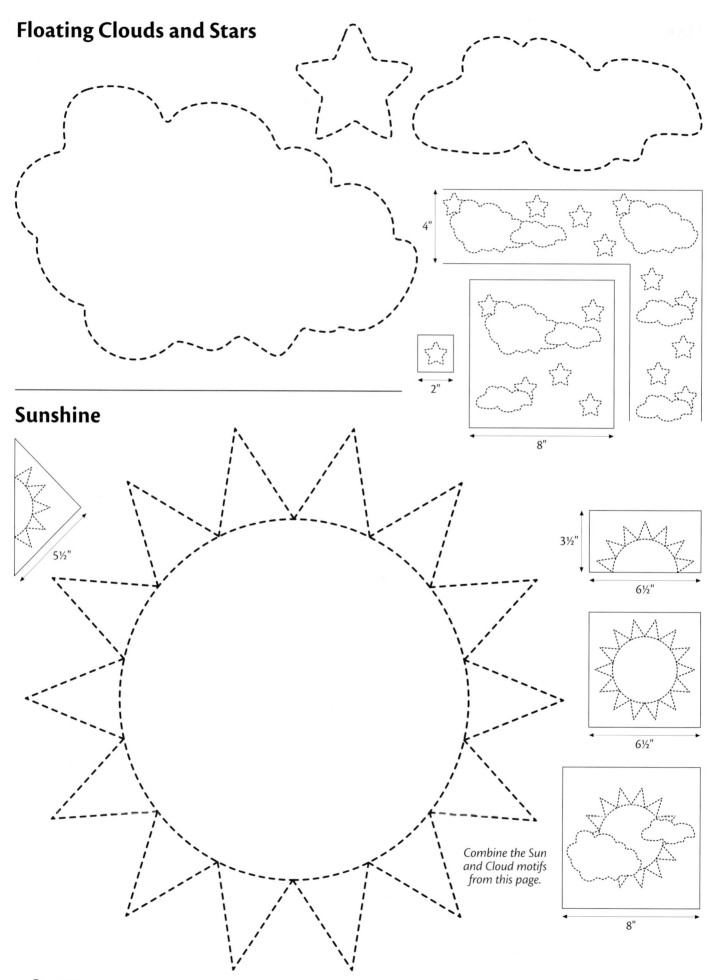

Sunshine

Combine the Sun and Cloud motifs from this page.

Man in the Moon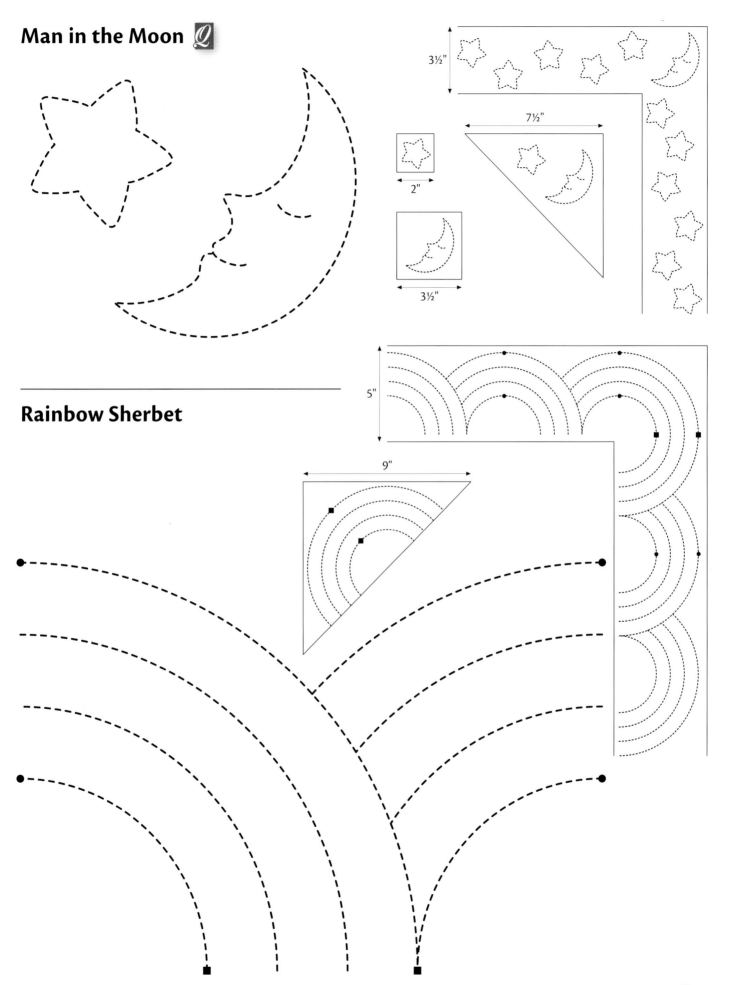

Rainbow Sherbet

Baby Birds

Teddy Bear

Reversed motifs are shown in gray.

Duck Stroll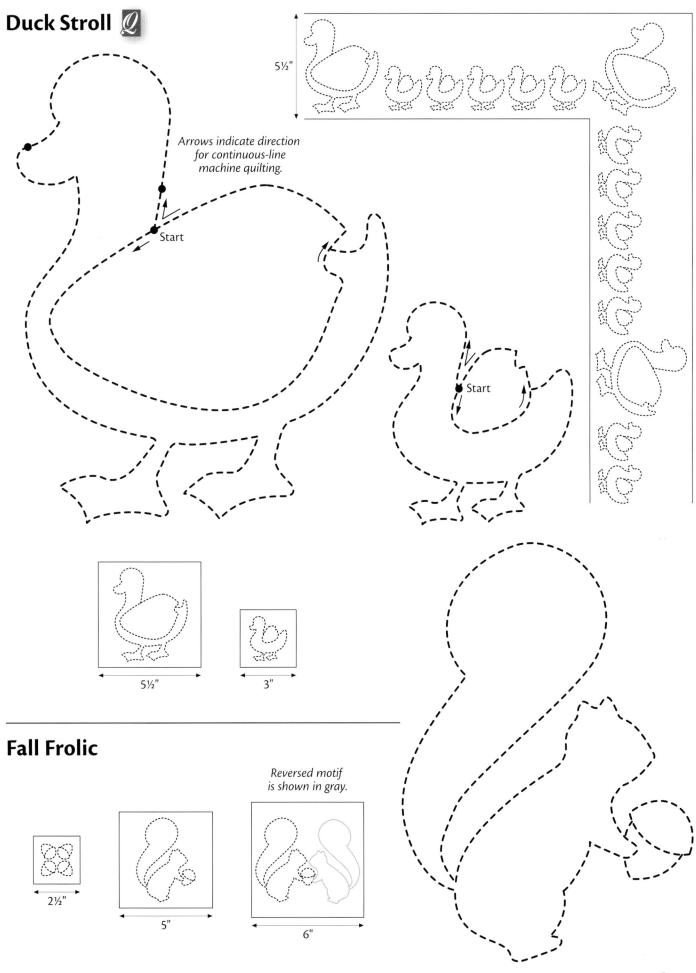

Arrows indicate direction for continuous-line machine quilting.

Start

Start

5½"

5½"

3"

Fall Frolic

Reversed motif is shown in gray.

2½"

5"

6"

Groovy Flowers

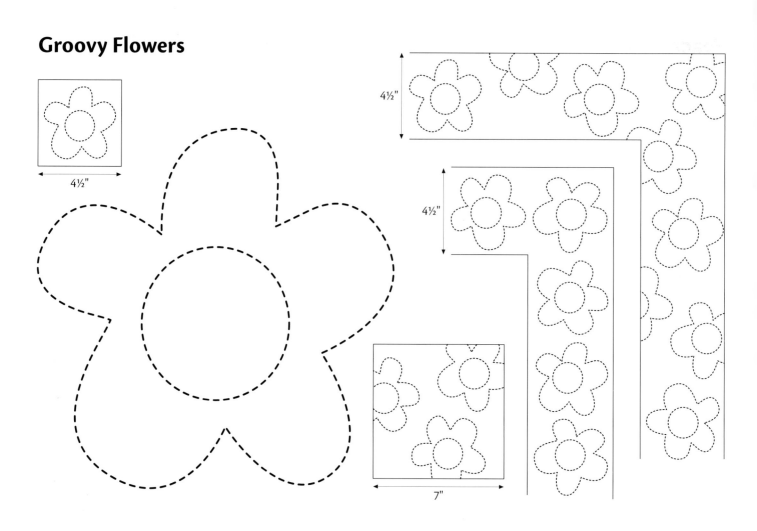

4½"

4½"

4½"

7"

Psychedelic Swirls

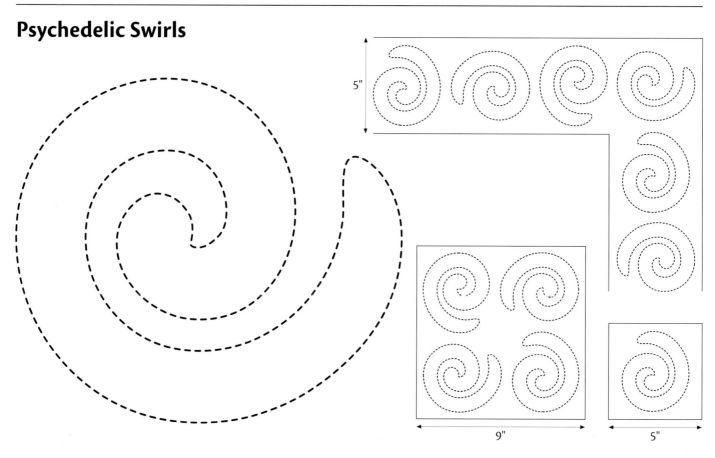

5"

9"

5"

Peace Sign

5"

5"

5"

Combine the '60s era designs from these two pages.

Happy Face

5"

5"

To the Moon

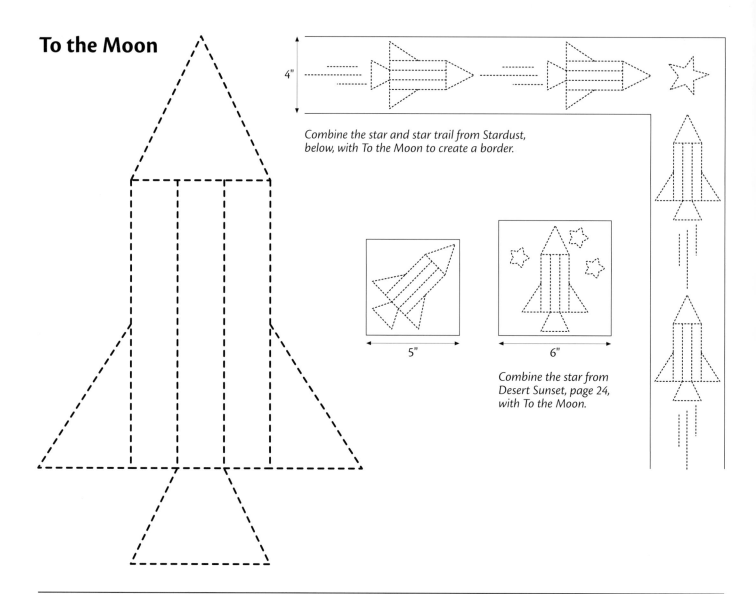

Combine the star and star trail from Stardust, below, with To the Moon to create a border.

Combine the star from Desert Sunset, page 24, with To the Moon.

Stardust

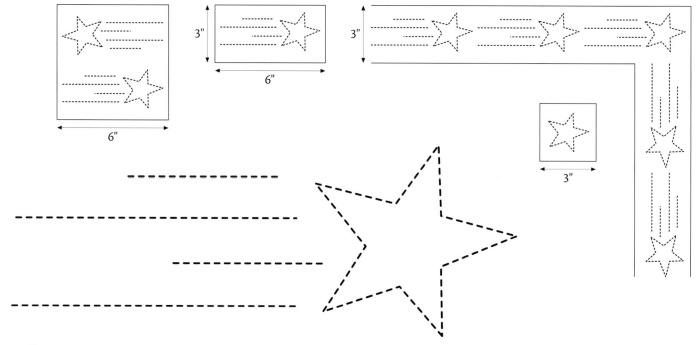

Sea Serpent/Knight

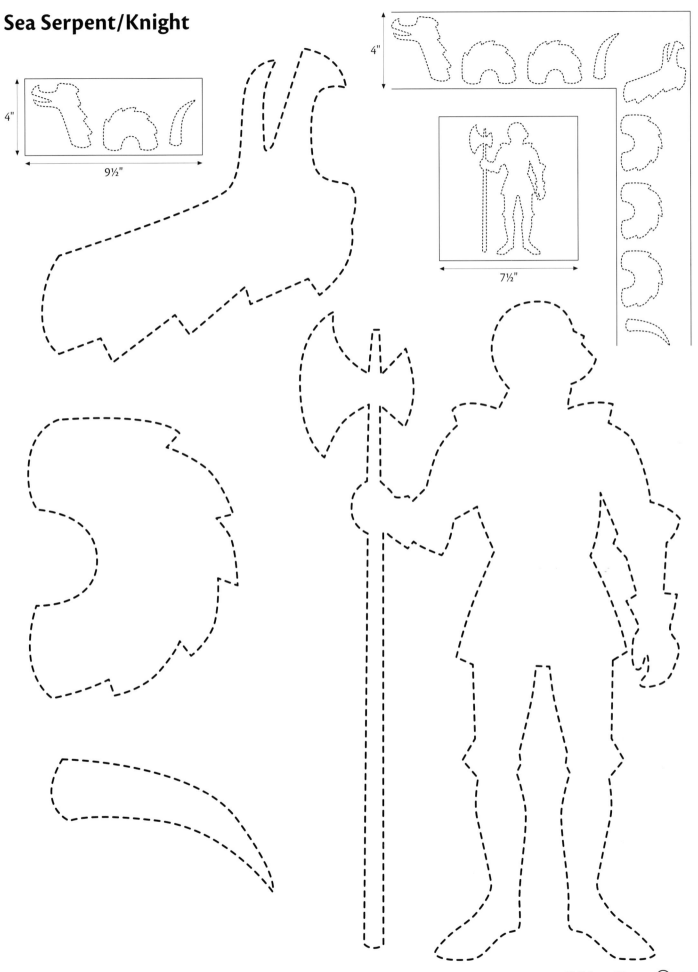

Flying Dragon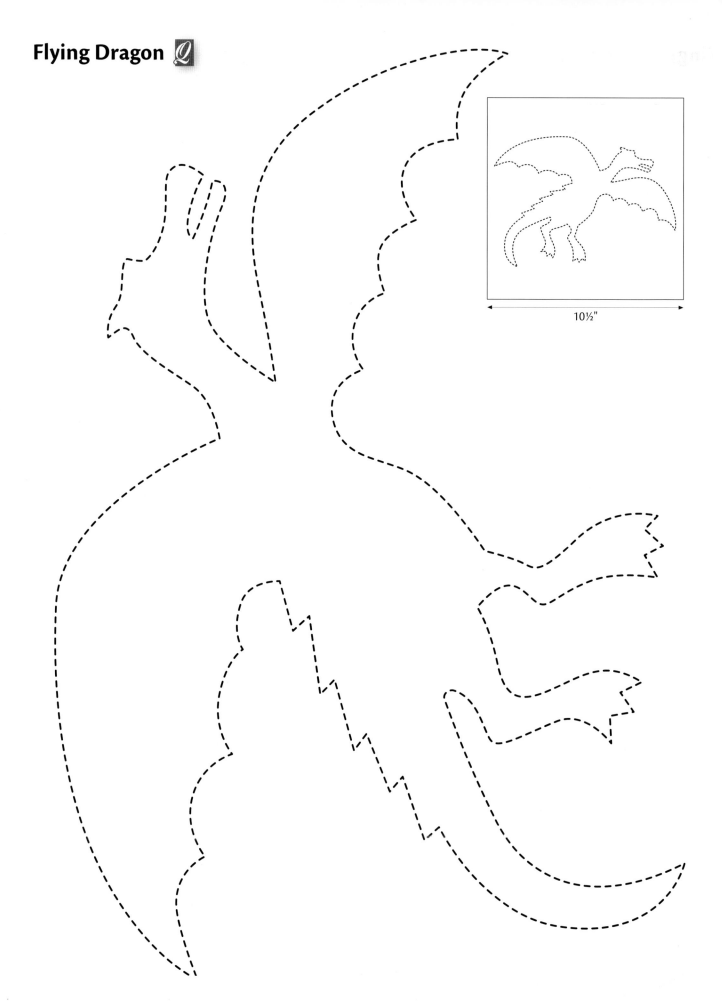

10½"

King/Princess

8½"

8½"

Castle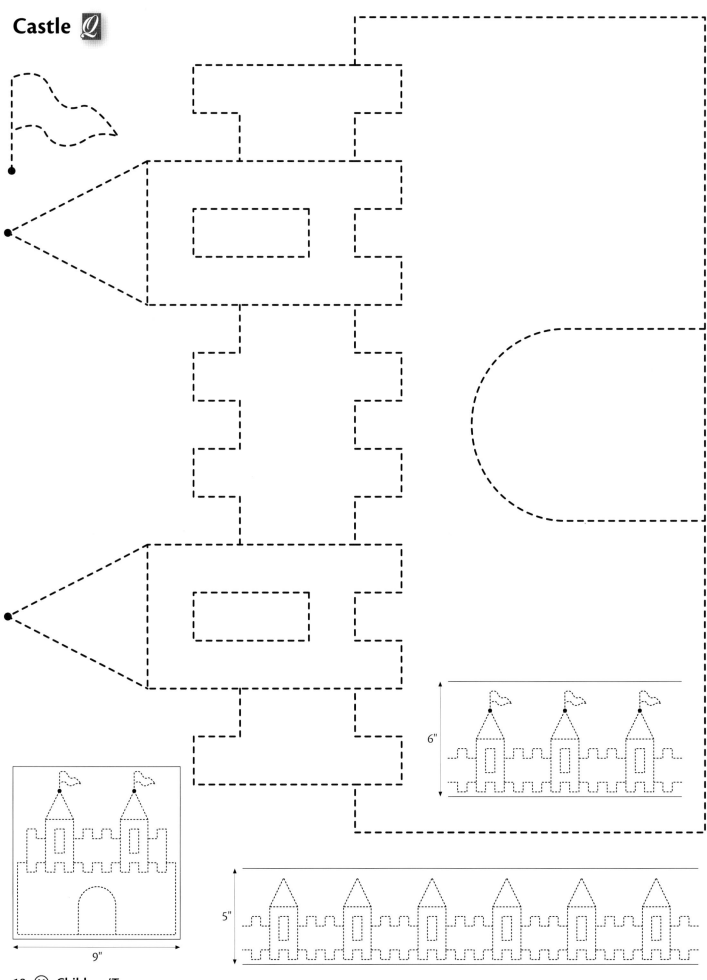

Unicorn/Horse

8½"

8½"

Elephants on Parade

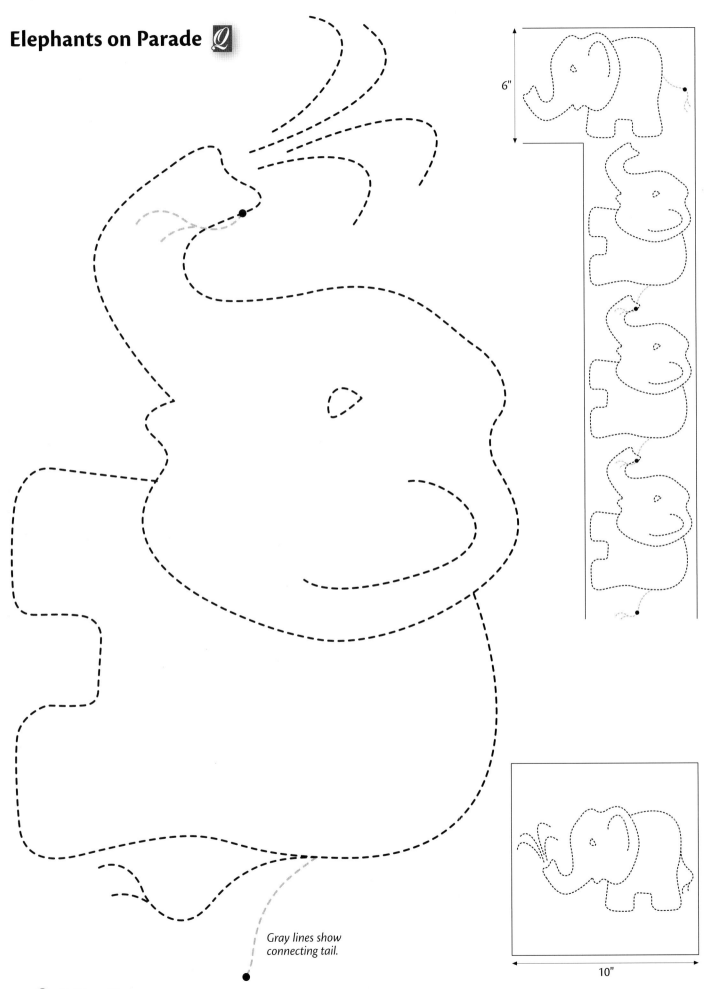

6"

Gray lines show connecting tail.

10"

Triple Scoop

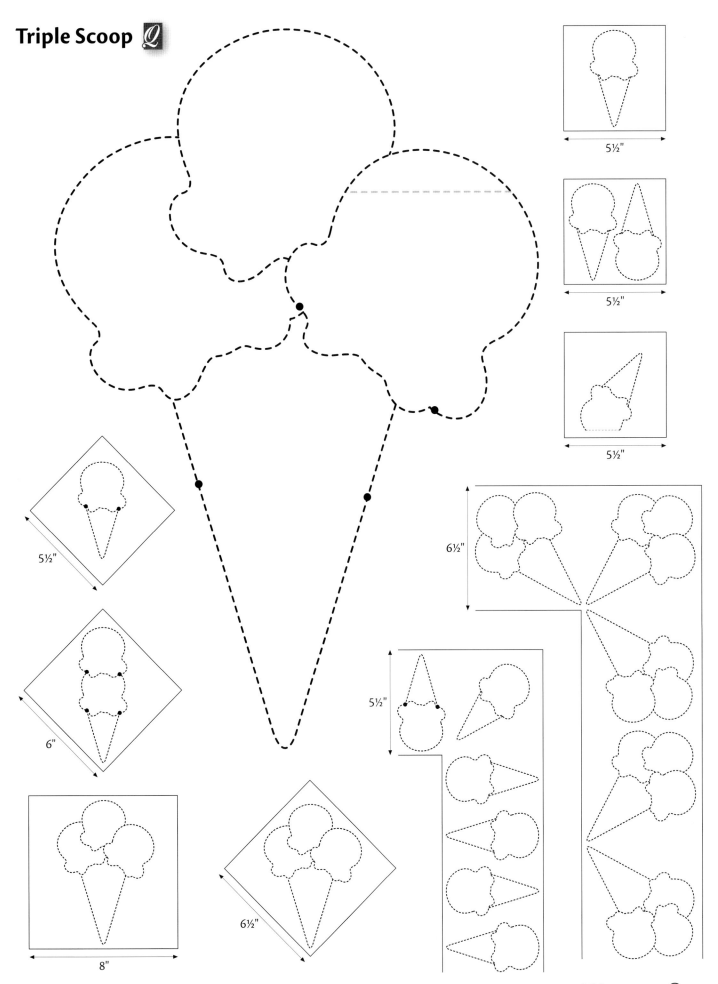

5½"

5½"

5½"

6½"

5½"

5½"

6"

6½"

8"

Best Foot Forward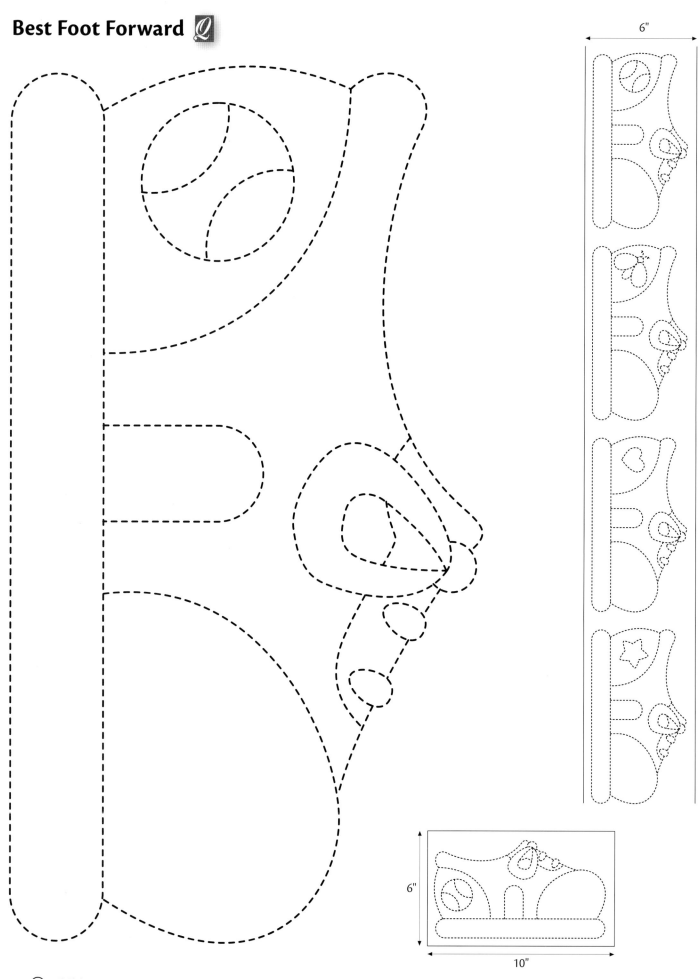

Twinkling Stars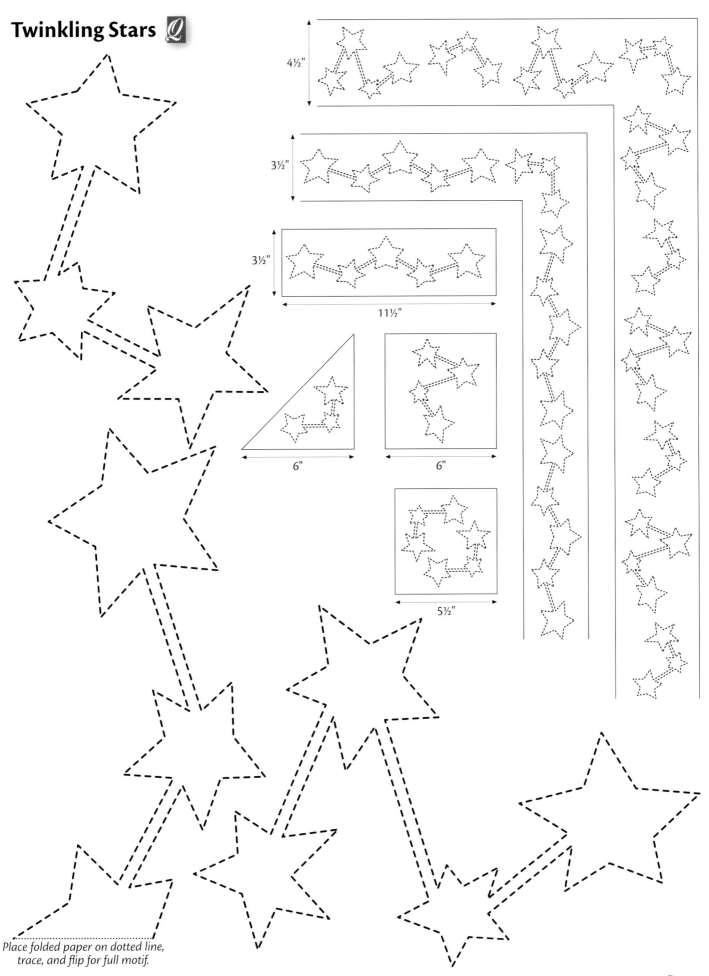

4½"

3½"

3½"

11½"

6"

6"

5½"

*Place folded paper on dotted line,
trace, and flip for full motif.*

Just Ducky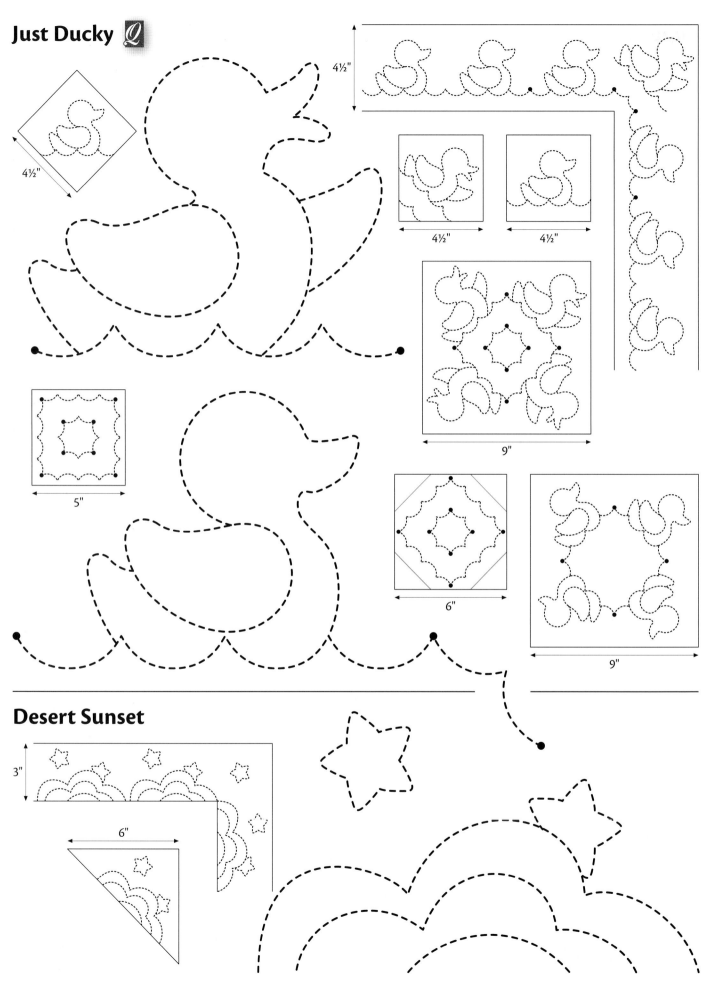

4½"

4½"

4½"

4½"

9"

5"

6"

9"

Desert Sunset

3"

6"

Puppy Romp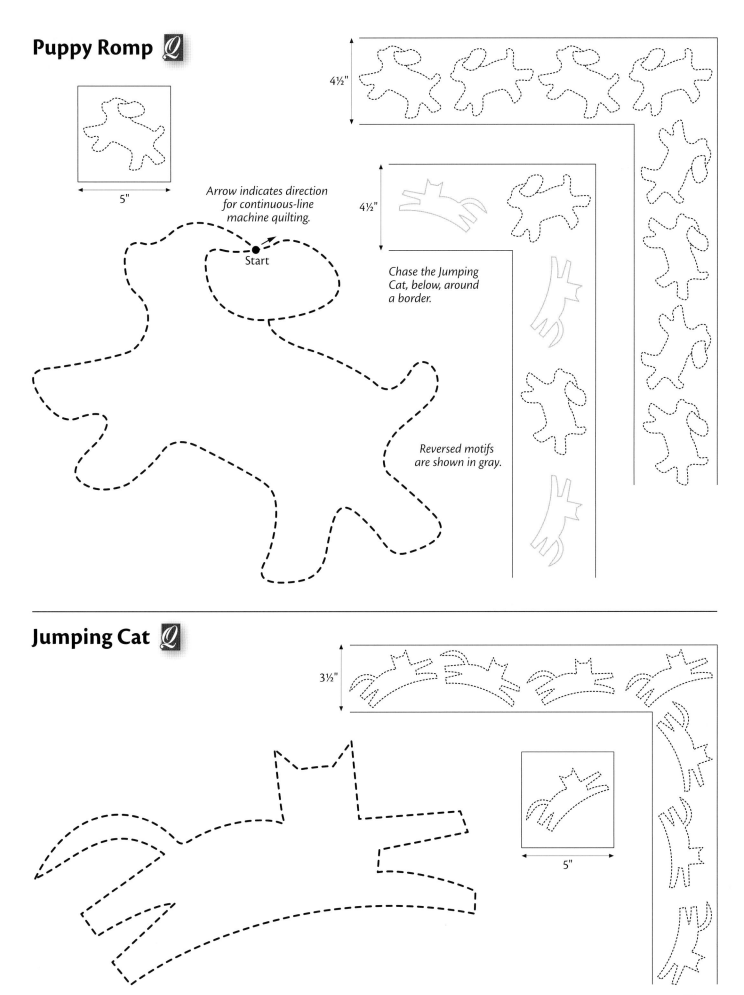

5"

Arrow indicates direction for continuous-line machine quilting.

Start

4½"

4½"

Chase the Jumping Cat, below, around a border.

Reversed motifs are shown in gray.

Jumping Cat

3½"

5"

Sheriff's Badge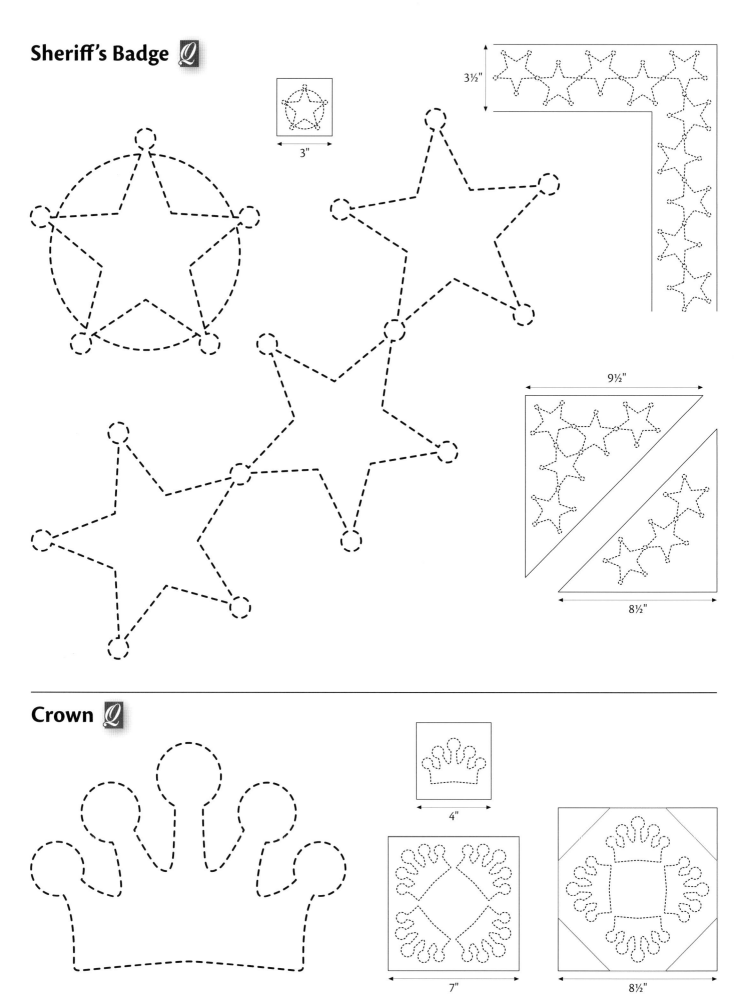

Crown

Bicycle

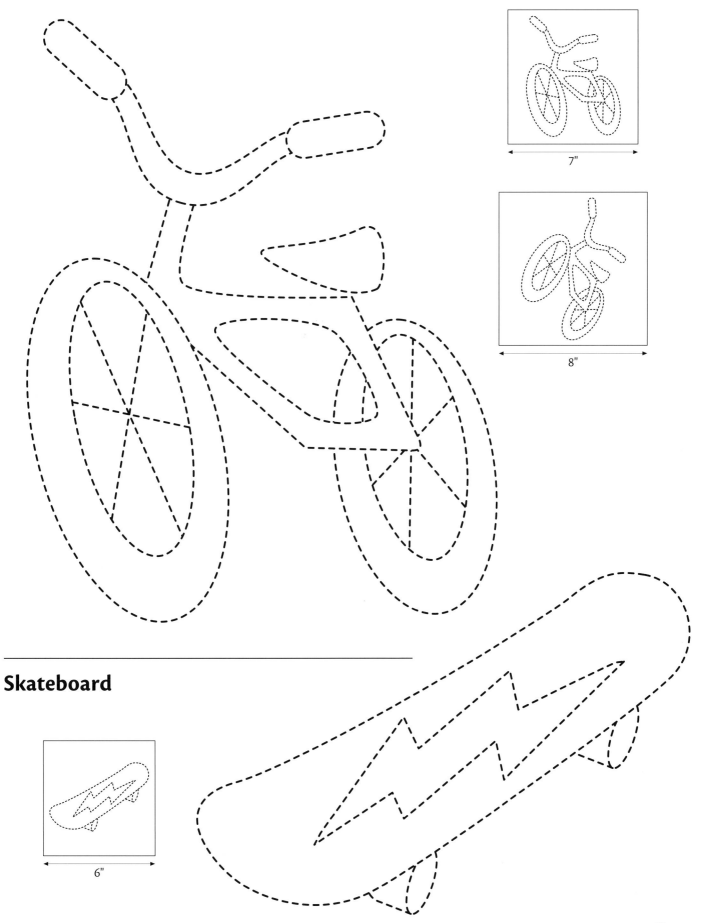

7"

8"

Skateboard

6"

Balloons

7½"

6½"

Bonnie Blue Ribbon

9½"

9"

6½"

2½"

12"

2½"

5"

2½"

4½"

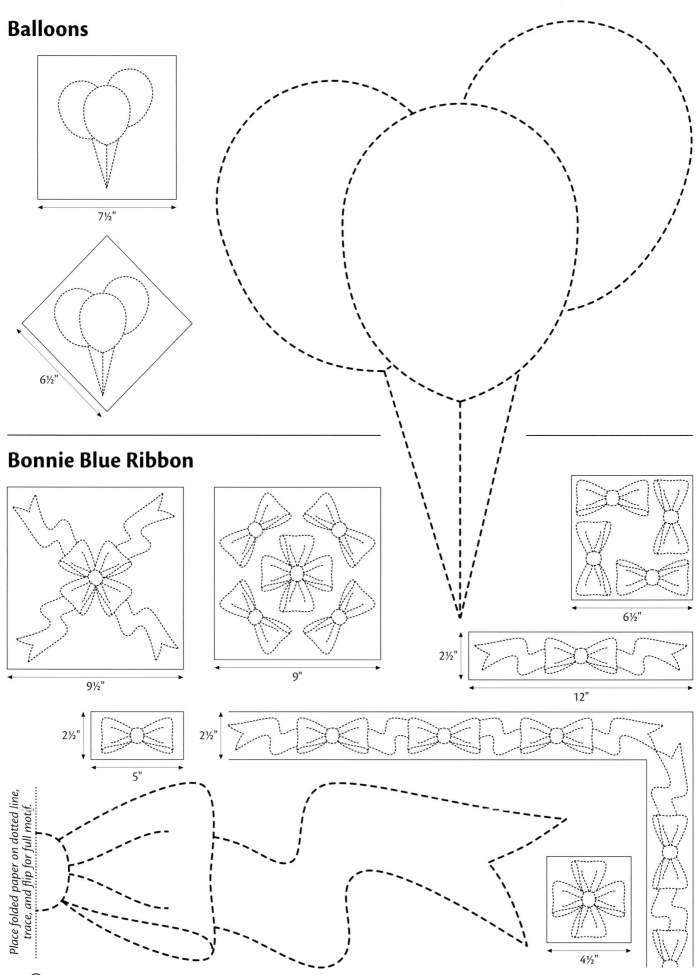

Place folded paper on dotted line, trace, and flip for full motif.

Two Bunnies

5½"

8"

5½"

Reversed motifs are shown in gray.

Butterfly

Shooting Stars

Penguin on Ice

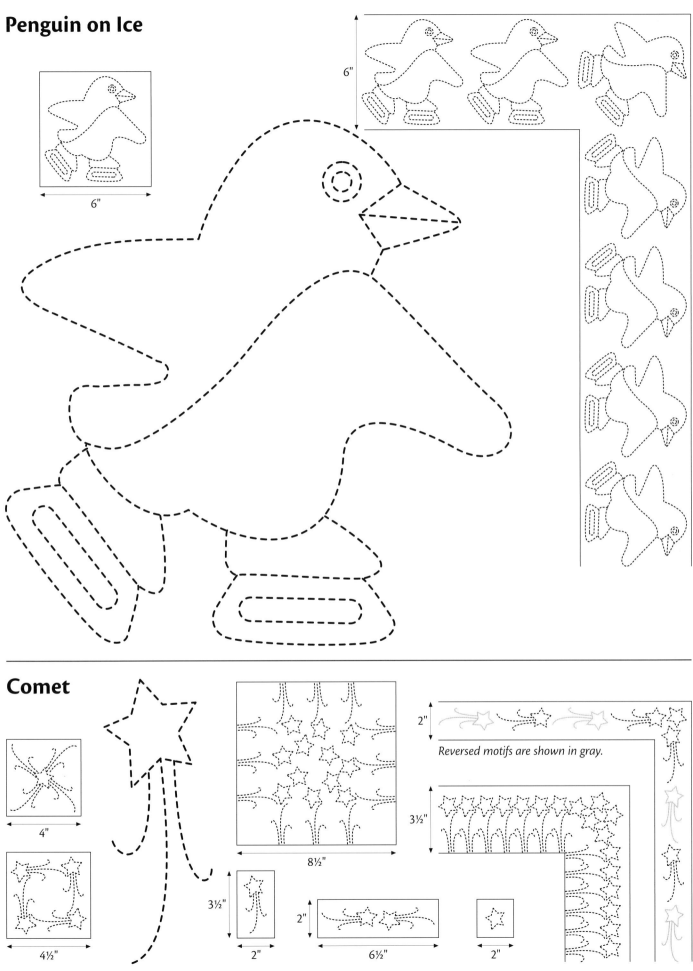

6"

6"

Comet

4"

4½"

3½"

2"

8½"

6½"

2"

2"

3½"

2"

Reversed motifs are shown in gray.

Little Star

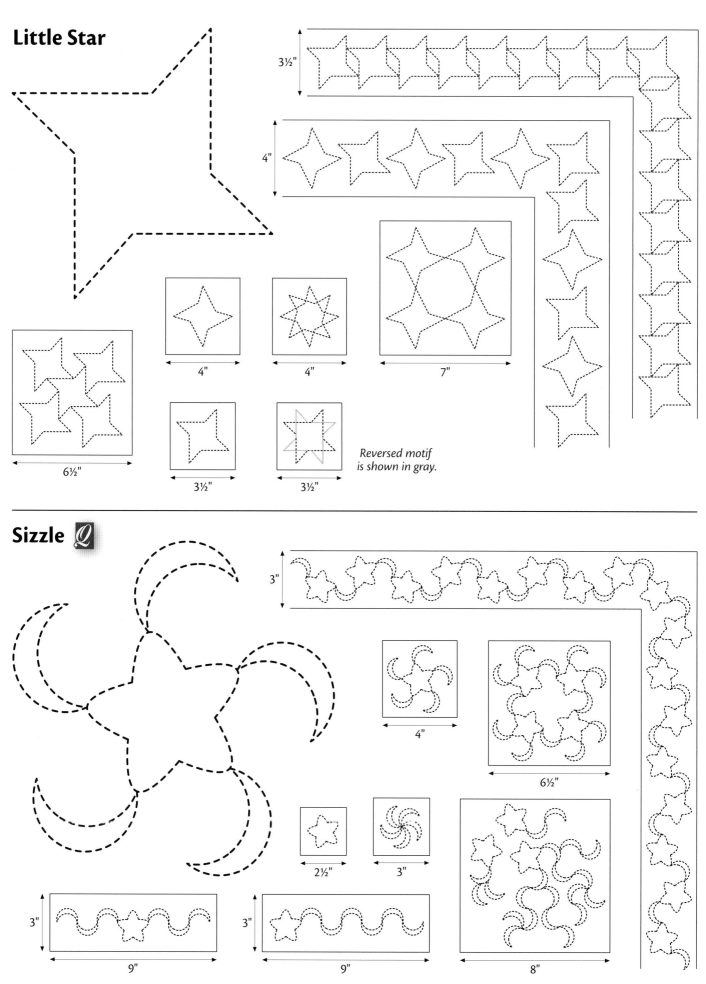

Reversed motif
is shown in gray.

3½"

4"

4"

4"

7"

6½"

3½"

3½"

Sizzle

3"

4"

6½"

2½"

3"

3"

9"

3"

9"

8"

Fizz Hearts

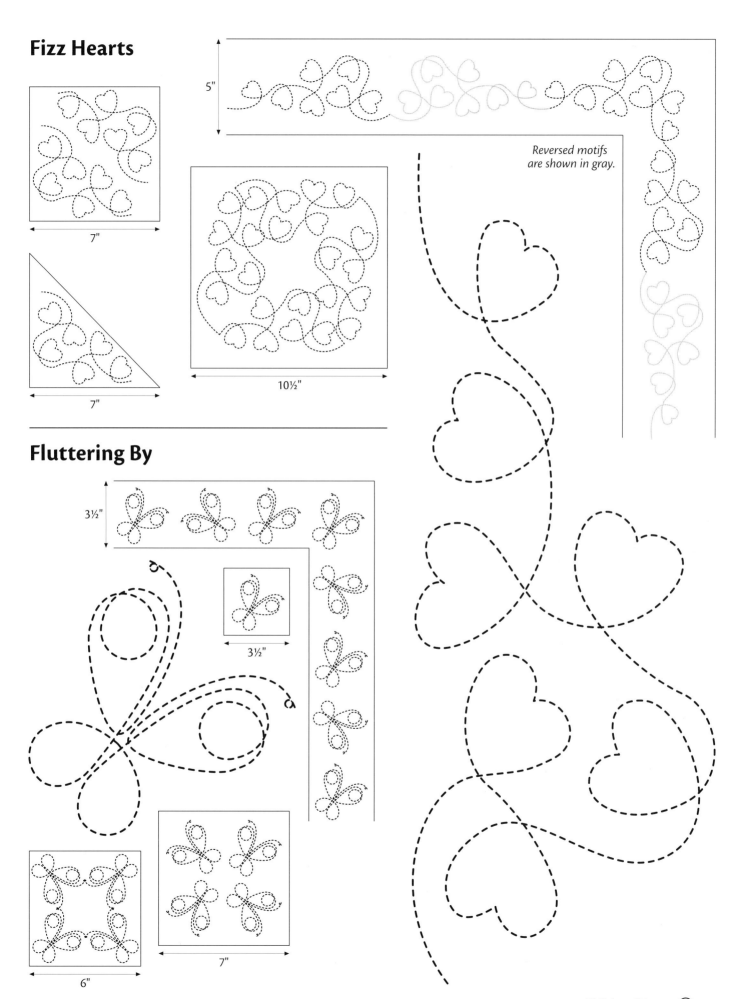

5"

Reversed motifs are shown in gray.

7"

7"

10½"

Fluttering By

3½"

3½"

7"

6"

Butterfly Dance

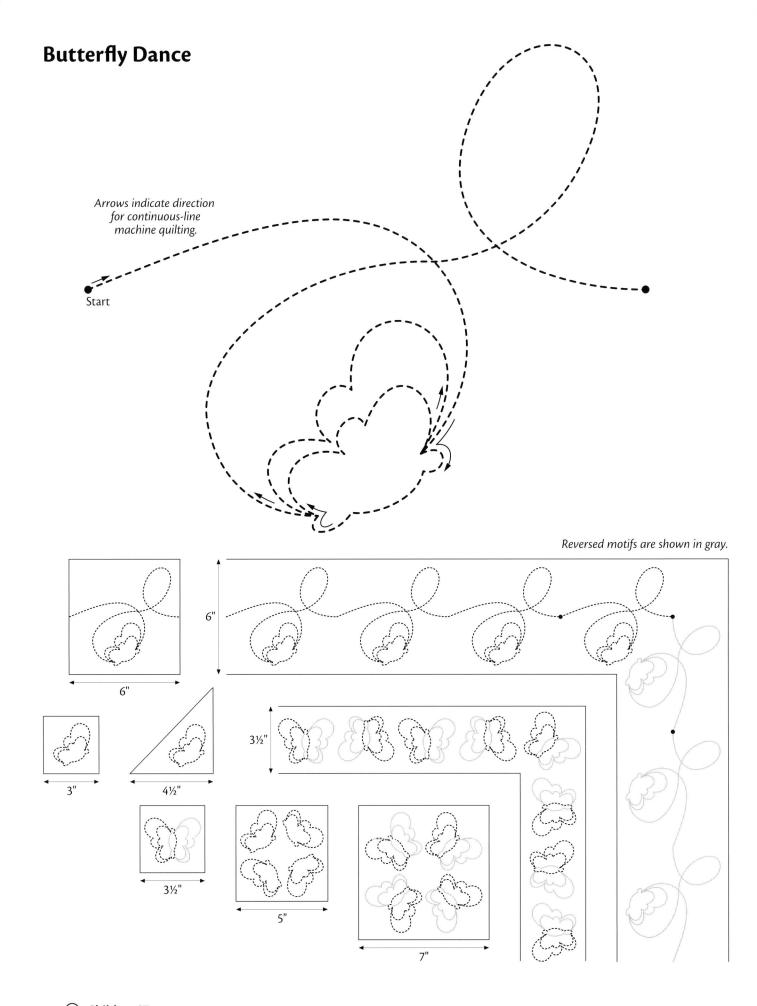

Arrows indicate direction for continuous-line machine quilting.

Start

Reversed motifs are shown in gray.

6"

6"

3½"

3"

4½"

3½"

5"

7"

Setting Sail

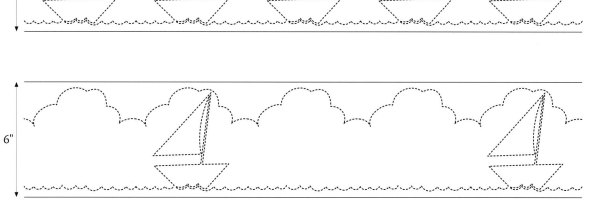

Dog Bone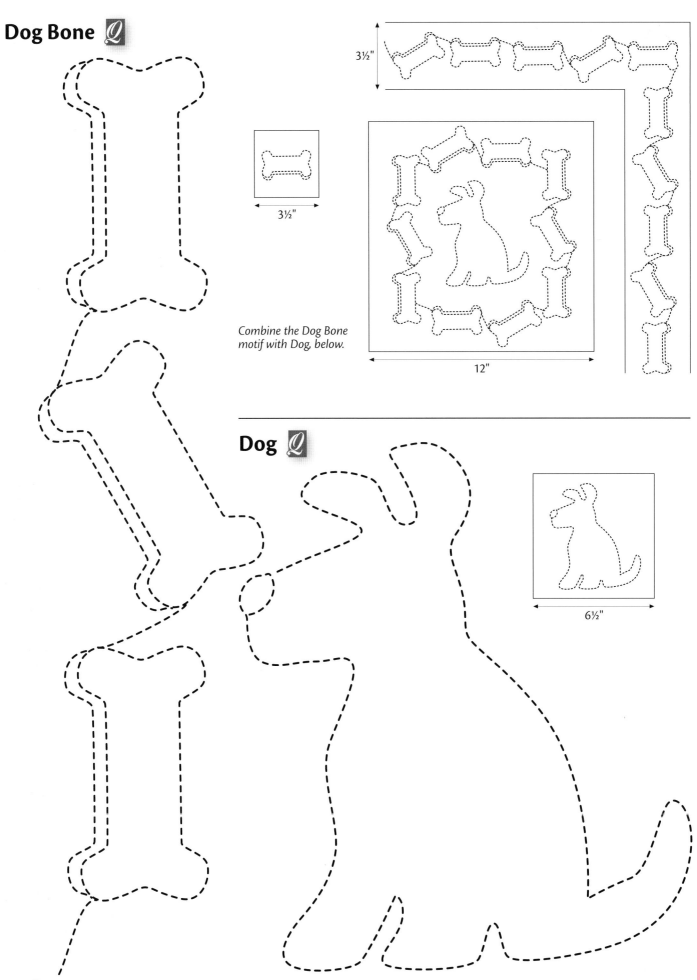

Combine the Dog Bone motif with Dog, below.

3½"

3½"

12"

Dog

6½"

Flying Colors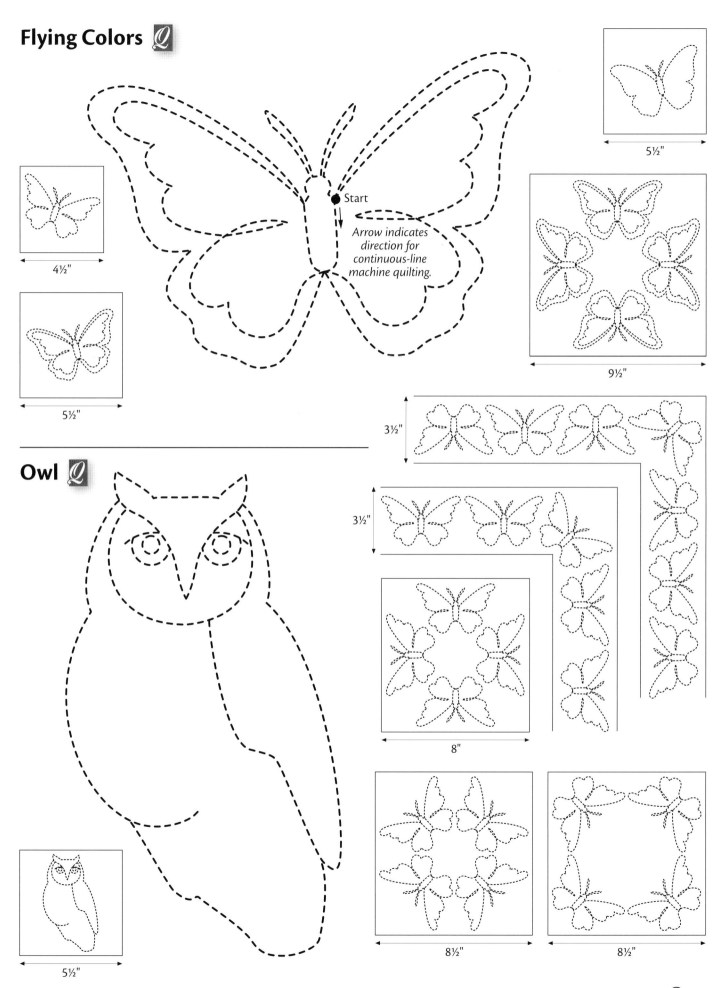

Start

Arrow indicates direction for continuous-line machine quilting.

4½"

5½"

5½"

9½"

3½"

3½"

8"

8½"

8½"

Owl

5½"

Feathers

Silver Plume

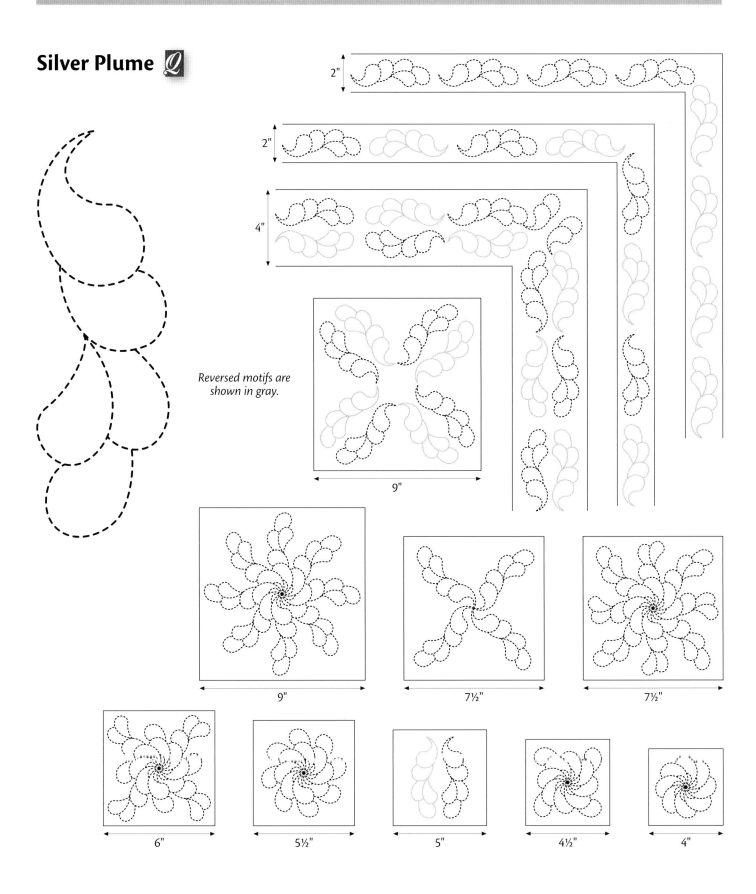

Reversed motifs are shown in gray.

2"

2"

4"

9"

9"

7½"

7½"

6"

5½"

5"

4½"

4"

Cocheco

5½"

6½"

4½"

7"

11"

9"

11"

Scalloped Teardrop

6"

5½"

6"

Start

Double Feather Wreath

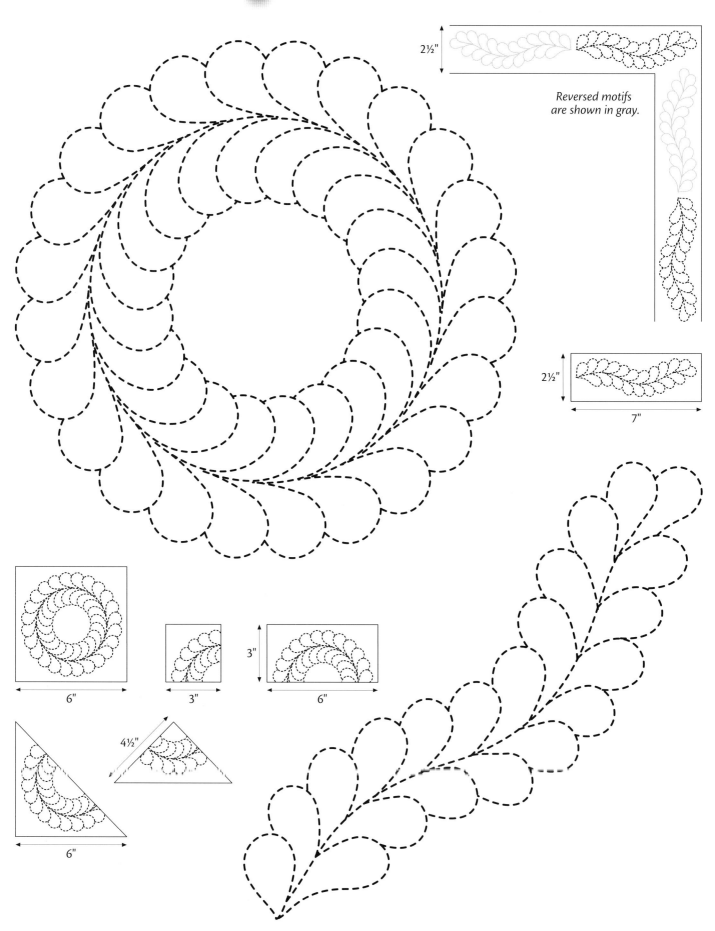

Reversed motifs
are shown in gray.

2½"

2½"

7"

6"

3"

3"

6"

6"

4½"

Fancy Feathers

Reversed motifs
are shown in gray.

9"

6½"

5"

3½"

13"

16"

Fanfare

Reversed motifs
are shown in gray.

4½"

4"

8½"

6½"

12"

15"

10"

12"

Feathered Cable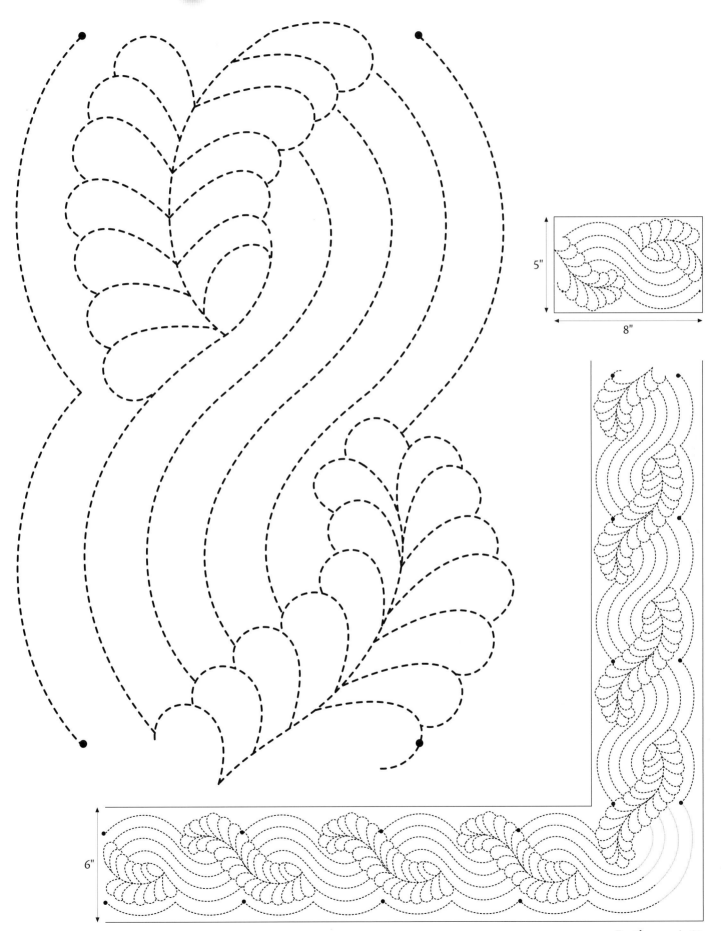

5"

8"

6"

Feather Heart

Place folded paper on dotted line, trace, and flip for full motif.

5"

9½"

9½"

6"

4"

17"

9½"

13½"

Feather Plume

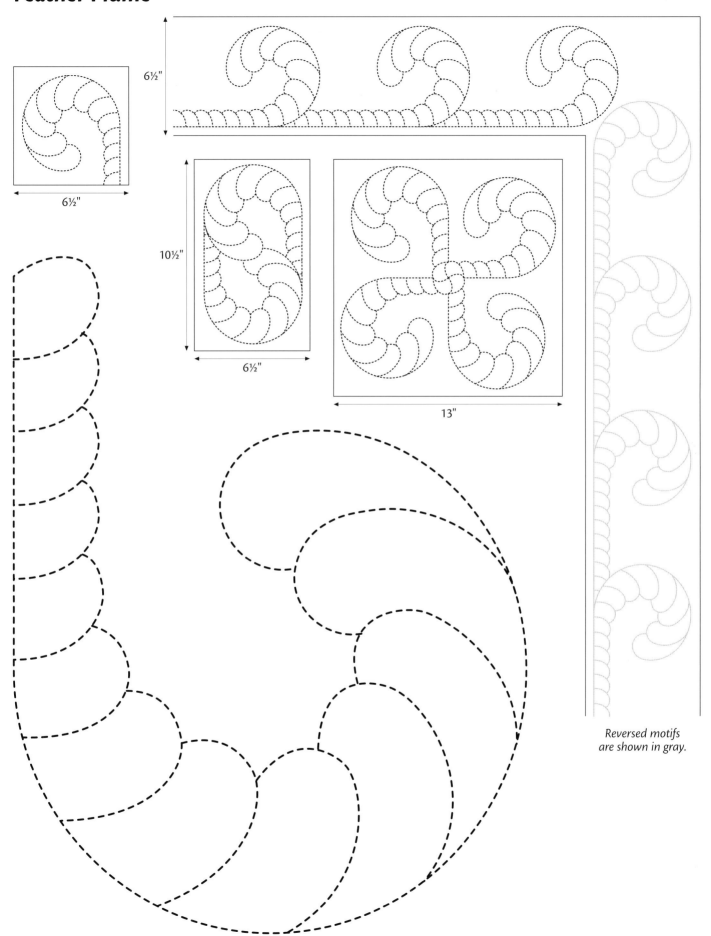

6½"

6½"

6½"

10½"

6½"

13"

Reversed motifs are shown in gray.

Feather Spray

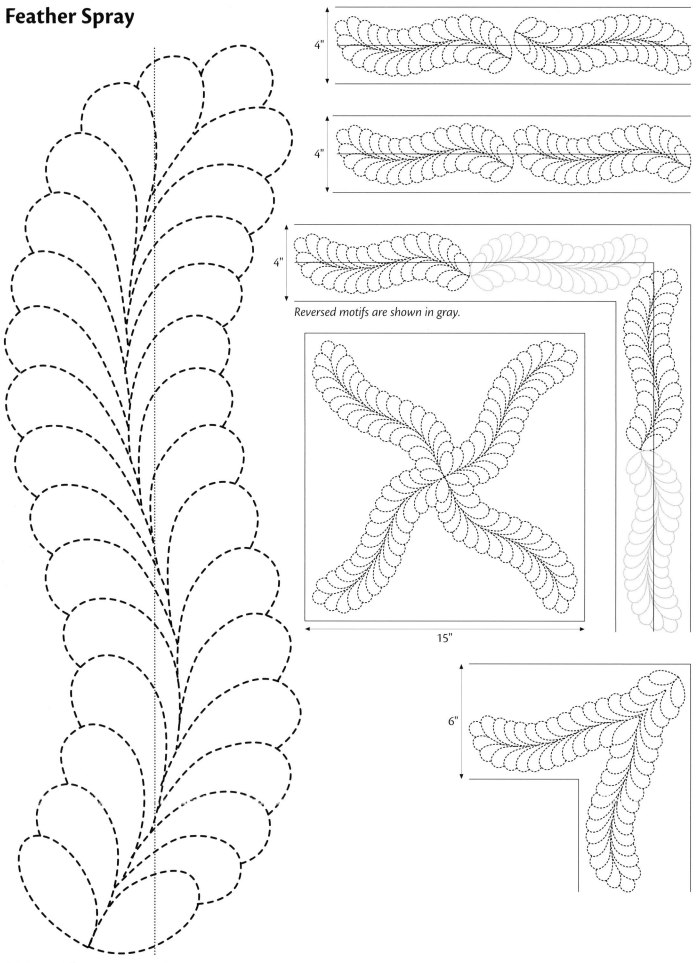

Reversed motifs are shown in gray.

4"

4"

4"

15"

6"

Feather Wreath 1

6"

7"

5½"

Center

Place folded paper on dotted lines, trace, and rotate for full motif.

11½"

11½"

12"

Feather Wreath 2

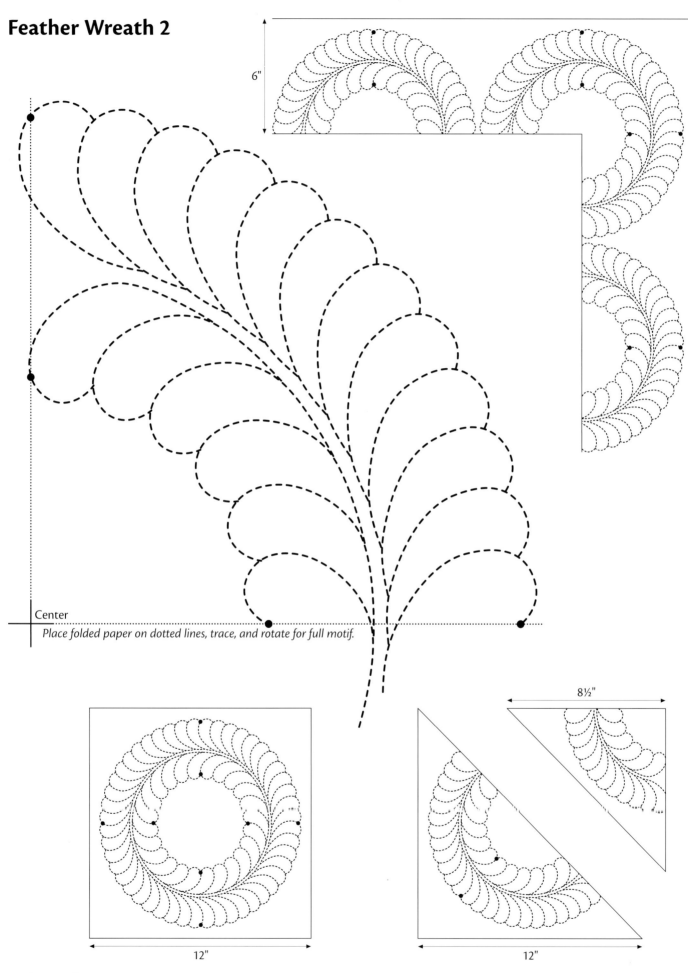

6"

Center

Place folded paper on dotted lines, trace, and rotate for full motif.

8½"

12"

12"

Goose Down

4½"

4½"

4½"

Reversed motifs are shown in gray.

Place folded paper on dotted line, trace, and rotate for full motif.

10½"

Kaleidoscope

Place folded paper on dotted line, trace, and flip for full motif.

5"

10"

13"

10"

8½"

9½"

9½"

Sun Feathers

Reversed motifs are shown in gray.

8½"

6"

13"

Sweethearts Q

Place folded paper on dotted line, trace, and flip for full motif.

5"

3½"

5½"

5"

10"

10½"

11"

Sweetheart Swag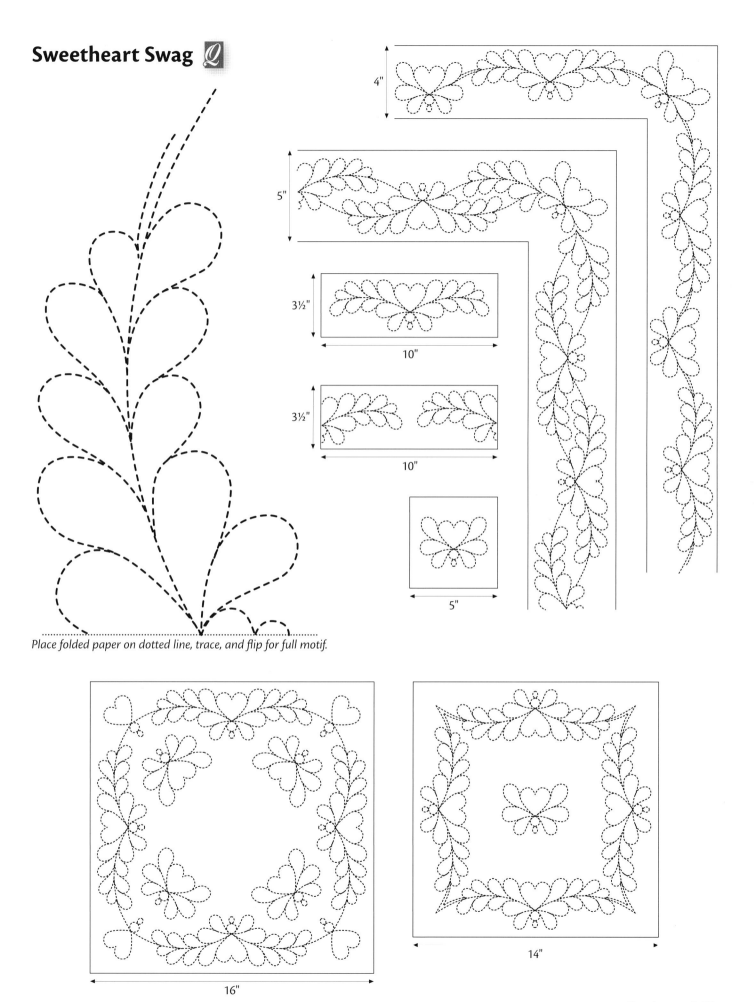

Place folded paper on dotted line, trace, and flip for full motif.

4"

5"

3½"

10"

3½"

10"

5"

16"

14"

Washington's Wreath

15"

11"

Center

Place folded paper on dotted lines, trace, and rotate for full motif.

Limerick Waves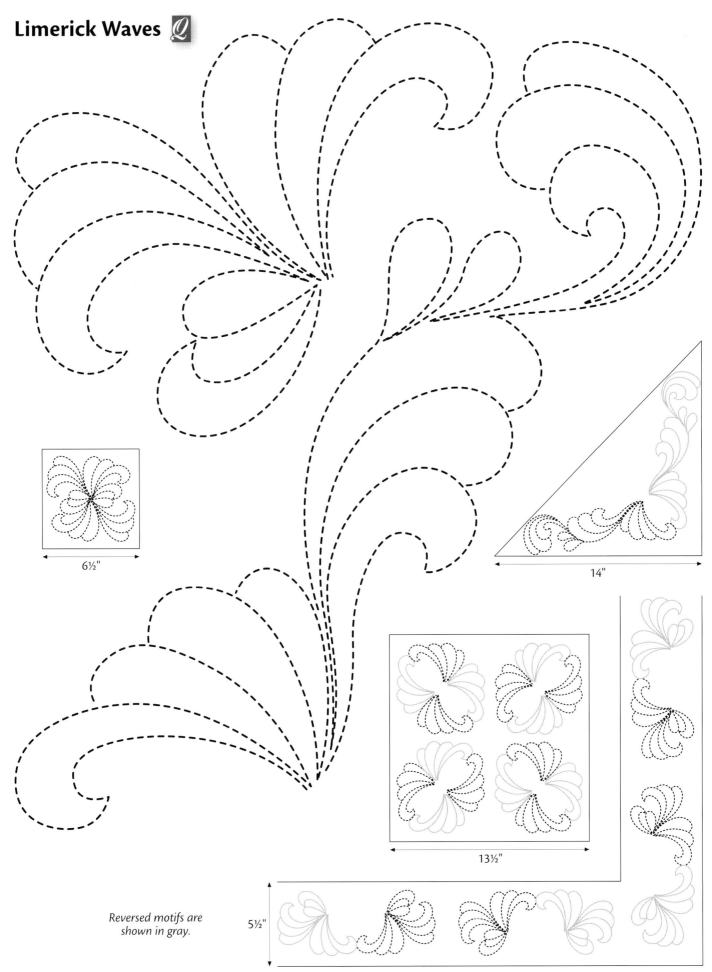

6½"

14"

13½"

5½"

*Reversed motifs are
shown in gray.*

Feathered Heart

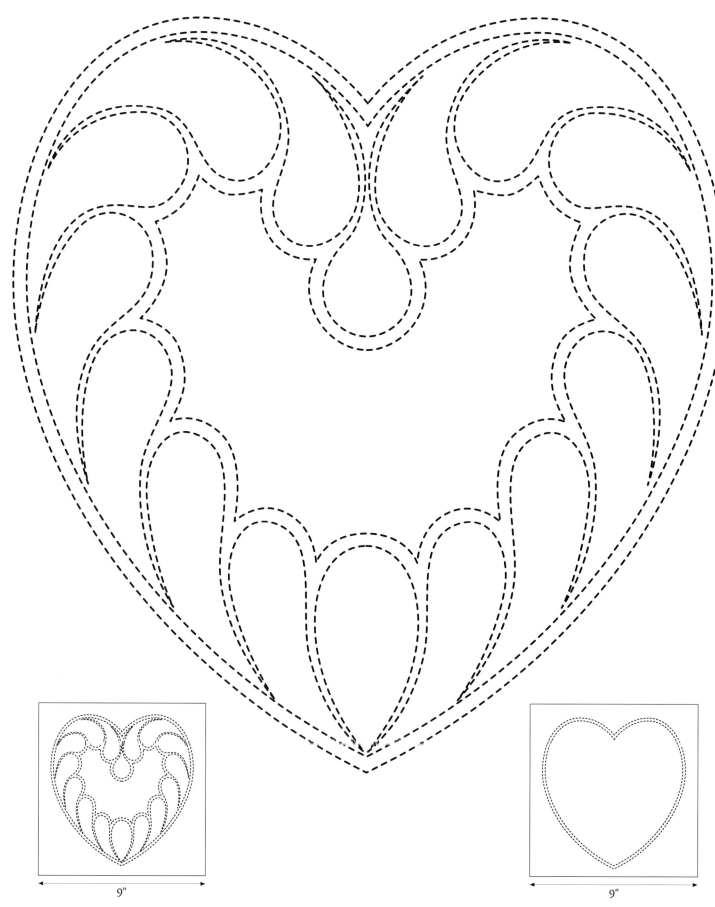

9"

9"

Feathered Heart

16"

17"

16"

10"

Sweet Talk

17"

9"

Reversed motifs are shown in gray.

7½"

Flowers

Celebration 1 Q

3"

3"

Reversed motifs
are shown in gray.

13"

7½"

6½"

4"

9½"

9½"

9½"

Lida Rose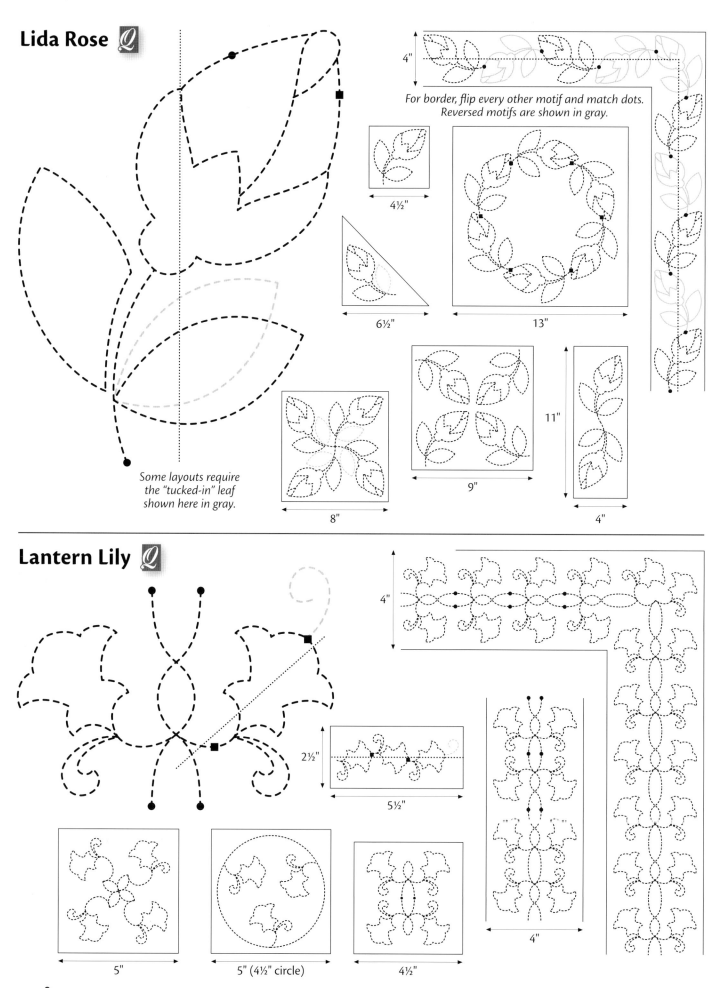

For border, flip every other motif and match dots.
Reversed motifs are shown in gray.

Some layouts require the "tucked-in" leaf shown here in gray.

4"

4½"

6½"

13"

8"

9"

11"

4"

Lantern Lily

2½"

5½"

4"

4"

5"

5" (4½" circle)

4½"

Wild Rose

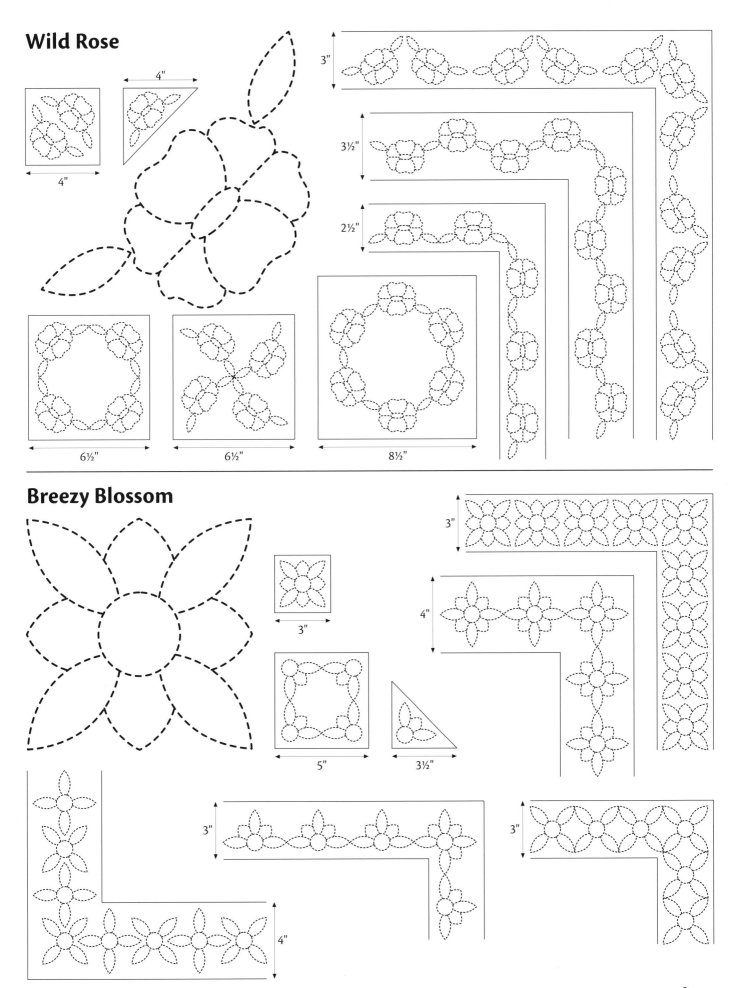

4"

4"

3"

3½"

2½"

6½"

6½"

8½"

Breezy Blossom

3"

5"

3½"

4"

3"

3"

3"

4"

Spring Promise

Reversed motifs are shown in gray.

Feathers and Flowers

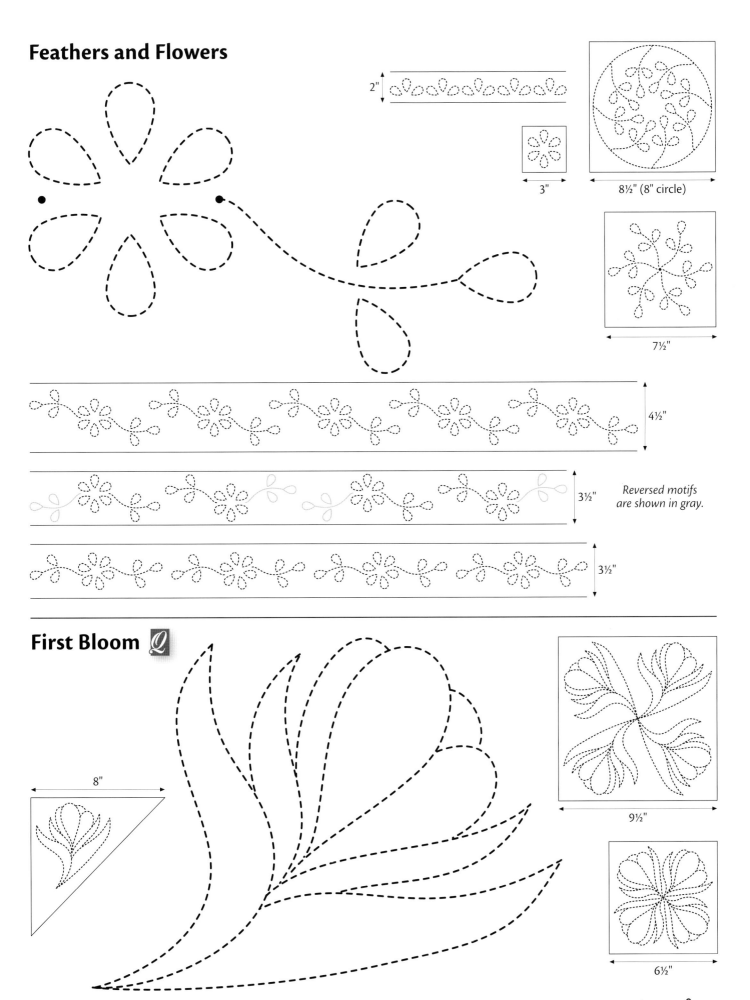

2"

3"

8½" (8" circle)

7½"

4½"

3½"

3½"

*Reversed motifs
are shown in gray.*

First Bloom

8"

9½"

6½"

He-Loves-Me

Arrows indicate direction for continuous-line machine quilting.

4½"

3"

3½"

5"

4½"

2"

2"

3"

9"

7"

6½"

6½"

Friendship Blossoms Q

Reversed motifs are shown in gray.

3"

3"

4"

3½"

5"

5½"

Rosebush Q

Reversed motifs are shown in gray.

3½"

7"

10½"

11½" (8½" circle)

11½" (8½" circle)

Floating Lily

10"

11"

4"

4"

6½"

8½"

5½"

5"

4½"

3½"

5"

Daisy Field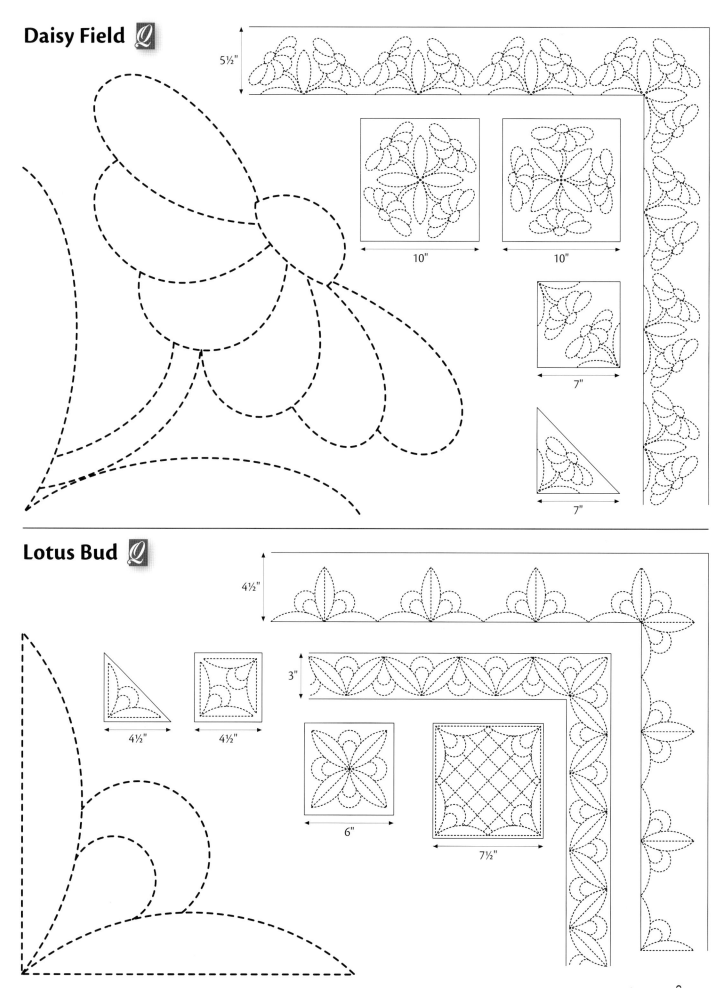

5½"

10"

10"

7"

7"

Lotus Bud

4½"

4½"

4½"

3"

6"

7½"

Persian Rose

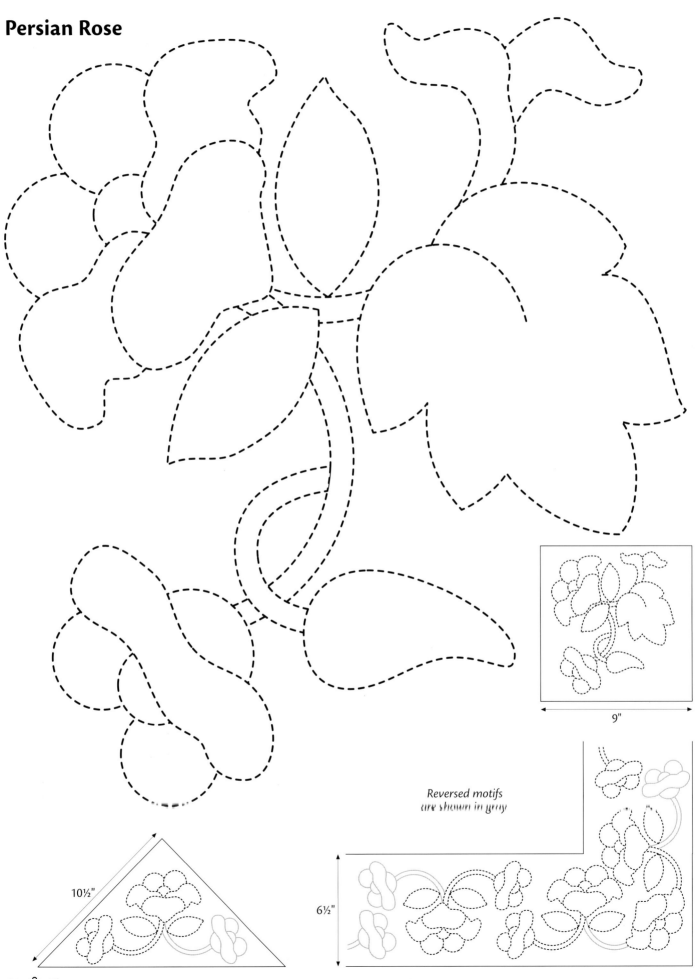

*Reversed motifs
are shown in gray*

9"

10½"

6½"

Floral Delight

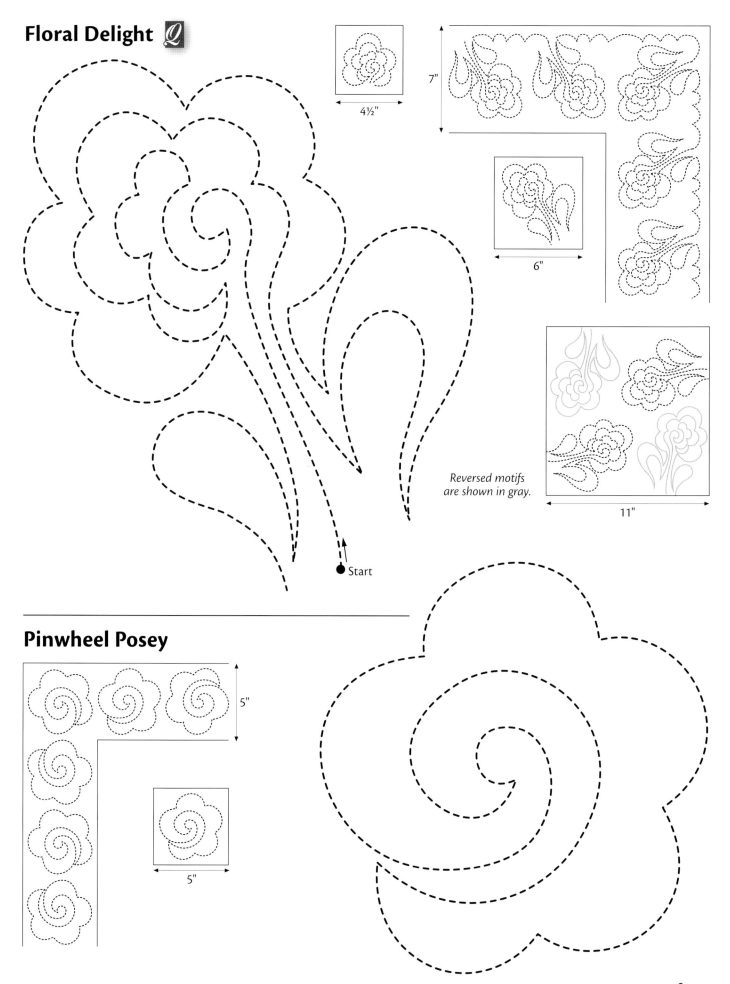

Reversed motifs are shown in gray.

4½"

7"

6"

11"

● Start

Pinwheel Posey

5"

5"

Tropical Fling

6"

12½"

9½"

13"

Arrows indicate direction for continuous-line machine quilting.

Start

End

Lily Bud

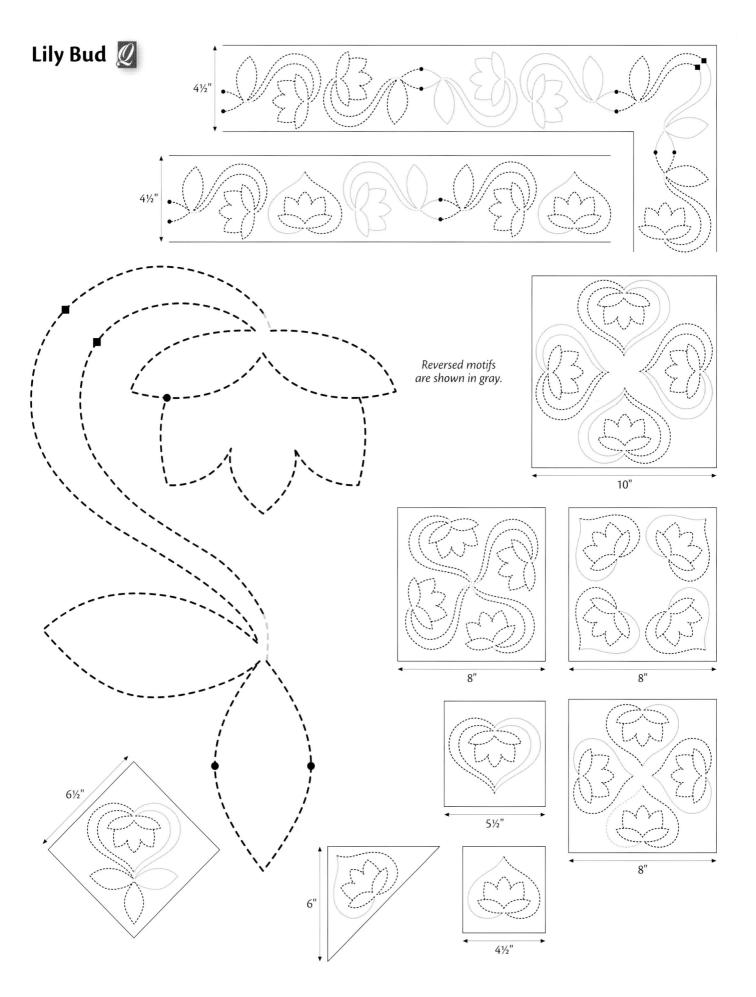

Reversed motifs
are shown in gray.

Jaunty Jump-Ups

8½" (7" circle)

6"

6½"

8½"

6"

5½" (4½" circle)

7"

7"

6"

3½"

6"

Harvest Bloom

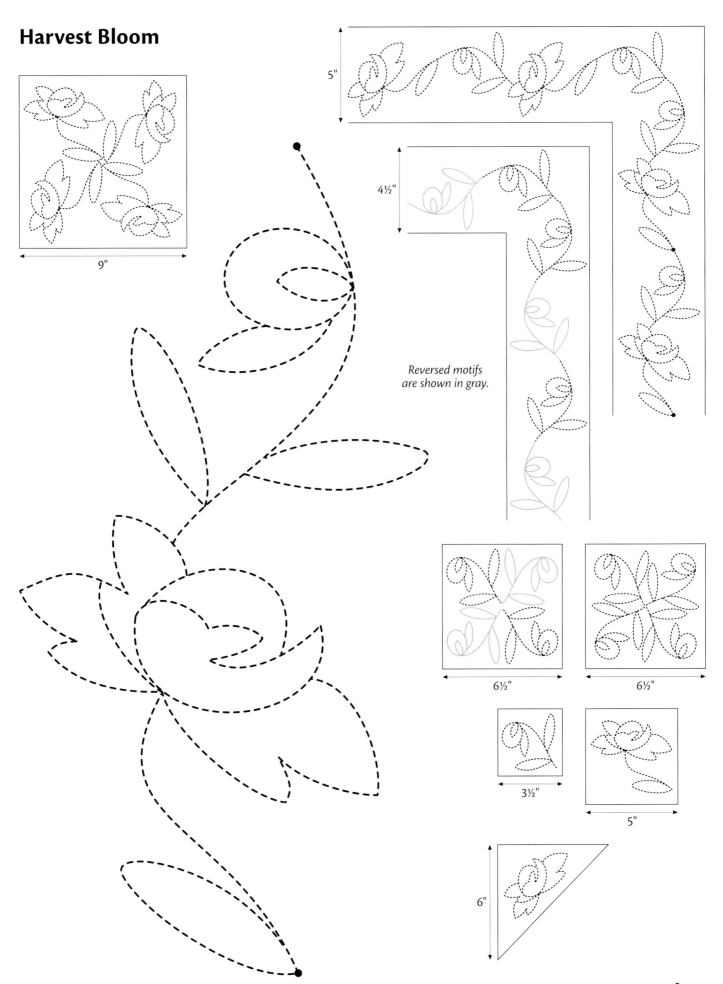

9"

5"

4½"

Reversed motifs are shown in gray.

6½"

6½"

3½"

5"

6"

Shasta Daisy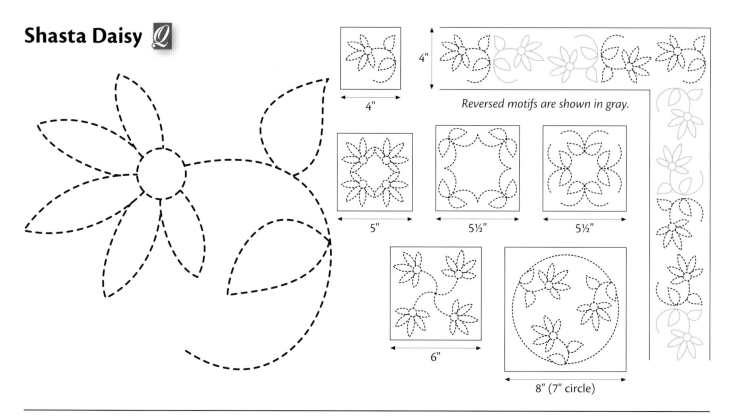

Reversed motifs are shown in gray.

4"

4"

5"

5½"

5½"

6"

8" (7" circle)

Silver Bells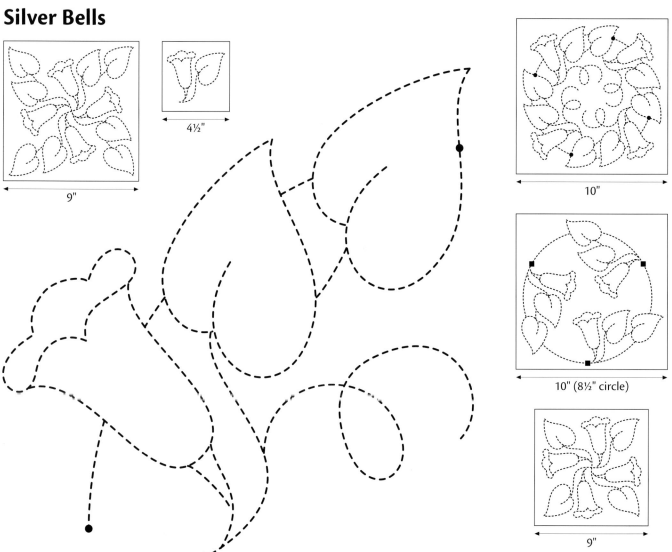

9"

4½"

10"

10" (8½" circle)

9"

Star Flower

5"

2½"

6½"

4½"

5"

4"

Springtime

3"

4½"

5"

2½"

3"

2½"

Rose Beauty

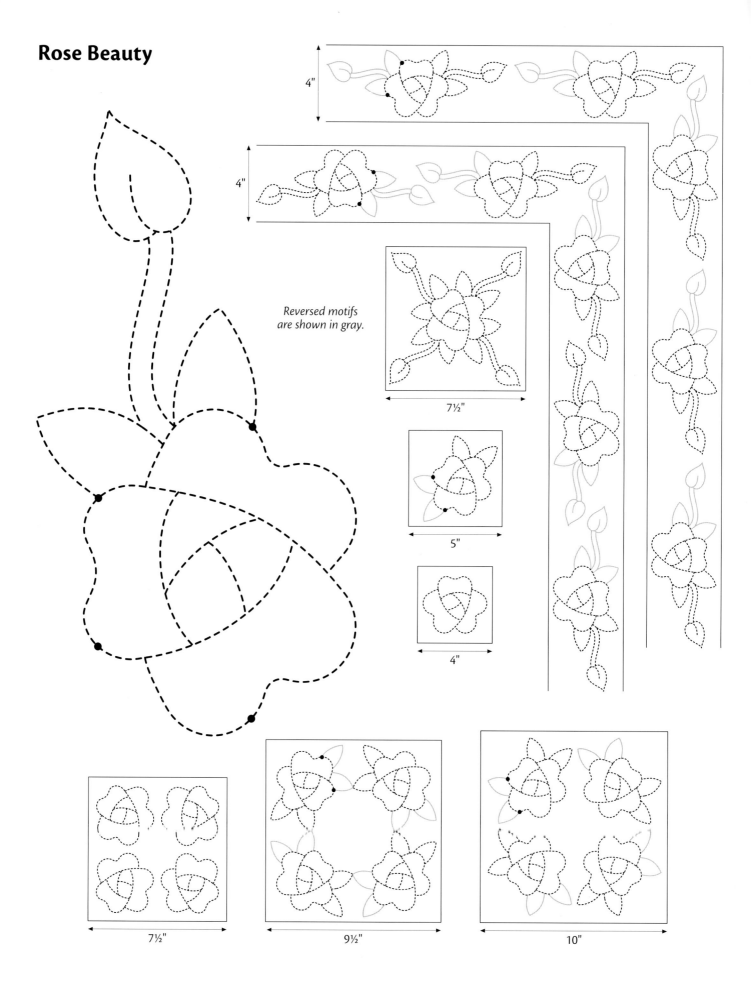

4"

4"

Reversed motifs
are shown in gray.

7½"

5"

4"

7½"

9½"

10"

Sparkling Flower

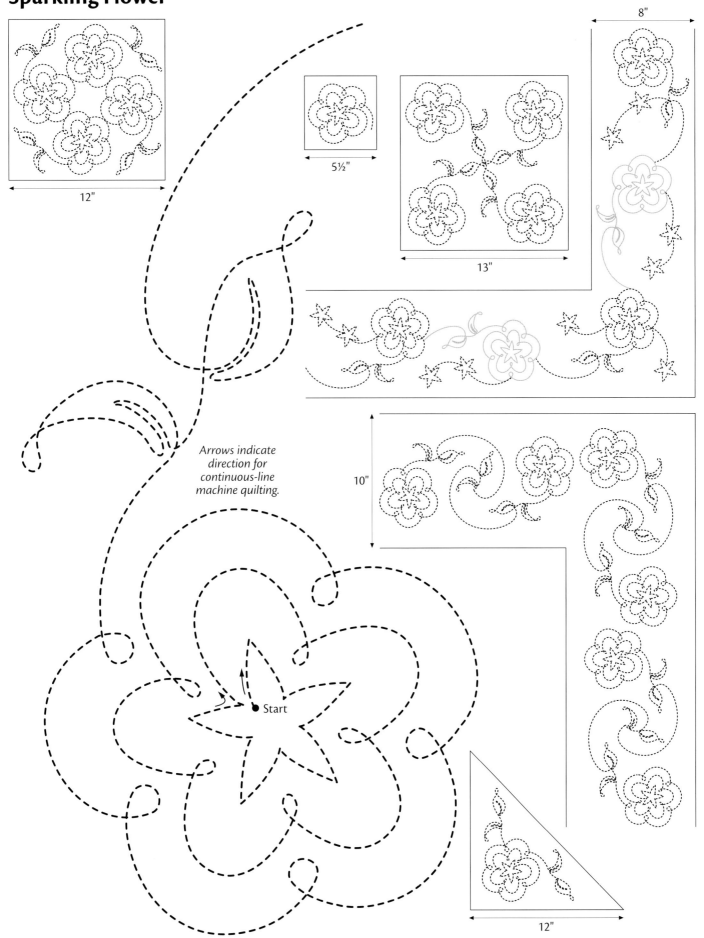

12"

5½"

13"

8"

10"

12"

Arrows indicate
direction for
continuous-line
machine quilting.

Start

Buttercup

Arrow indicates direction for continuous-line machine quilting.

Start

3"

3"   5"   3"

4"   5"

Flower of Youth

5"

9½"

3"

8"

3"   6"   7"

Happy Days

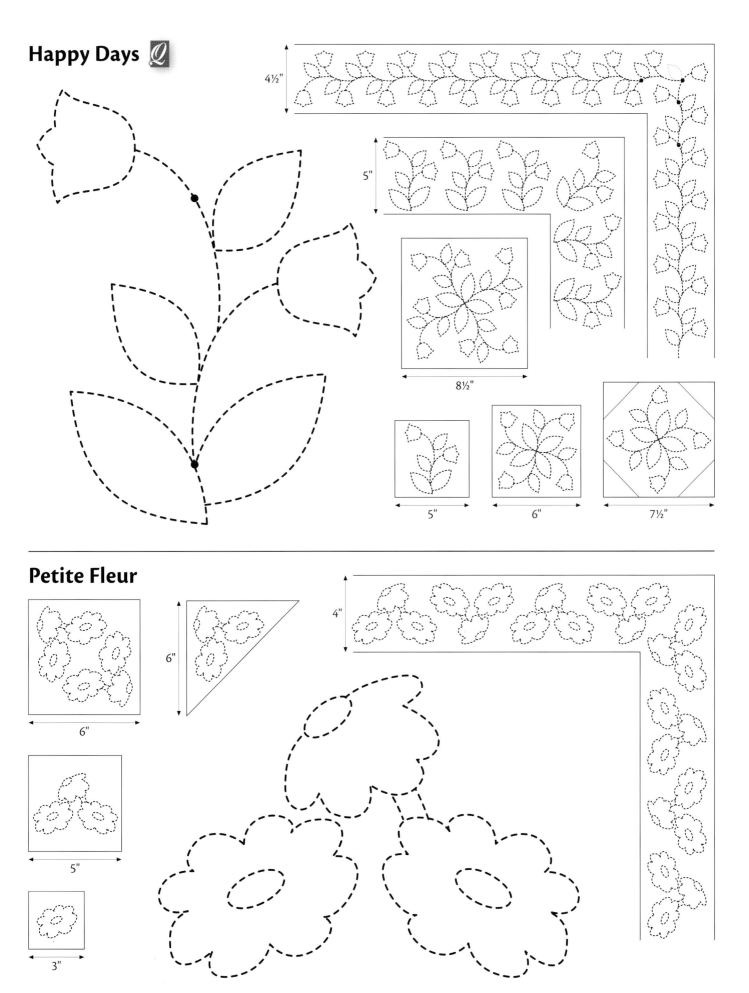

Petite Fleur

Belle Fleur

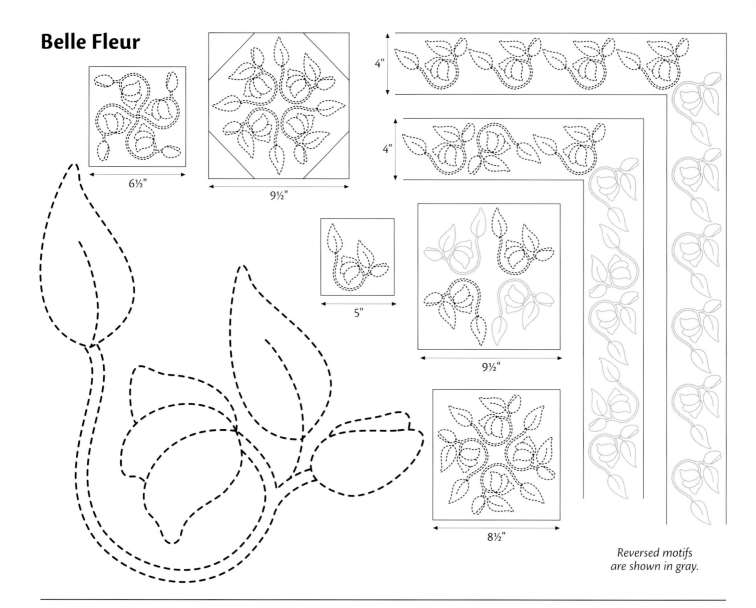

6½"

9½"

4"

4"

5"

9½"

8½"

*Reversed motifs
are shown in gray.*

Daisy Delight

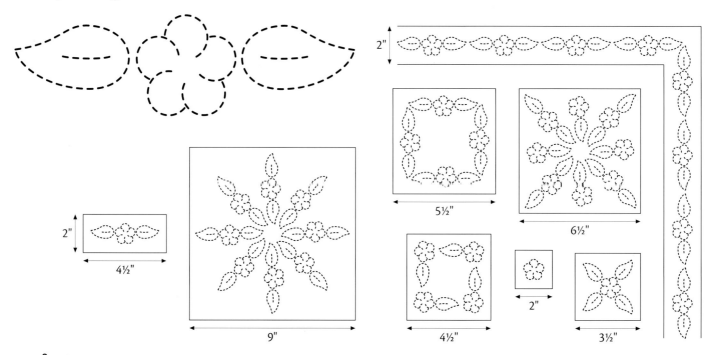

2"

2"

4½"

9"

5½"

6½"

4½"

2"

3½"

Grandma's Trellis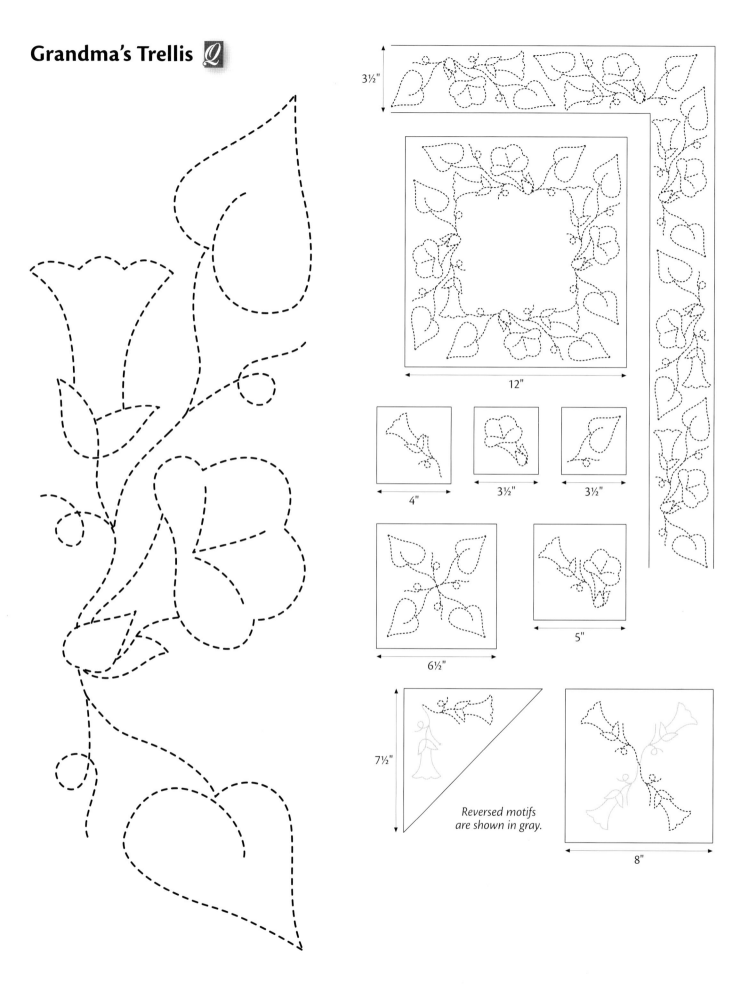

3½"

12"

4"

3½"

3½"

6½"

5"

7½"

8"

*Reversed motifs
are shown in gray.*

Shy Violet

Reversed motif
is shown in gray.

5"

7"

7"

4"

7"

3"

9½"

6½"

Budding Beauty

6½"

7"

4½"

3"

3"

3"

8½"

10"

7"

Reversed motifs
are shown in gray.

8½"

8½" (5½" circle)

8½"

Place folded paper on dotted lines, trace, and rotate for full motif.

Center

Evening Flower

Place folded paper on dotted lines, trace, and rotate for full motif.

Center

3"

5½"

6"

6"

8½"

17"

12½"

12½"

4½"

Floral Spray

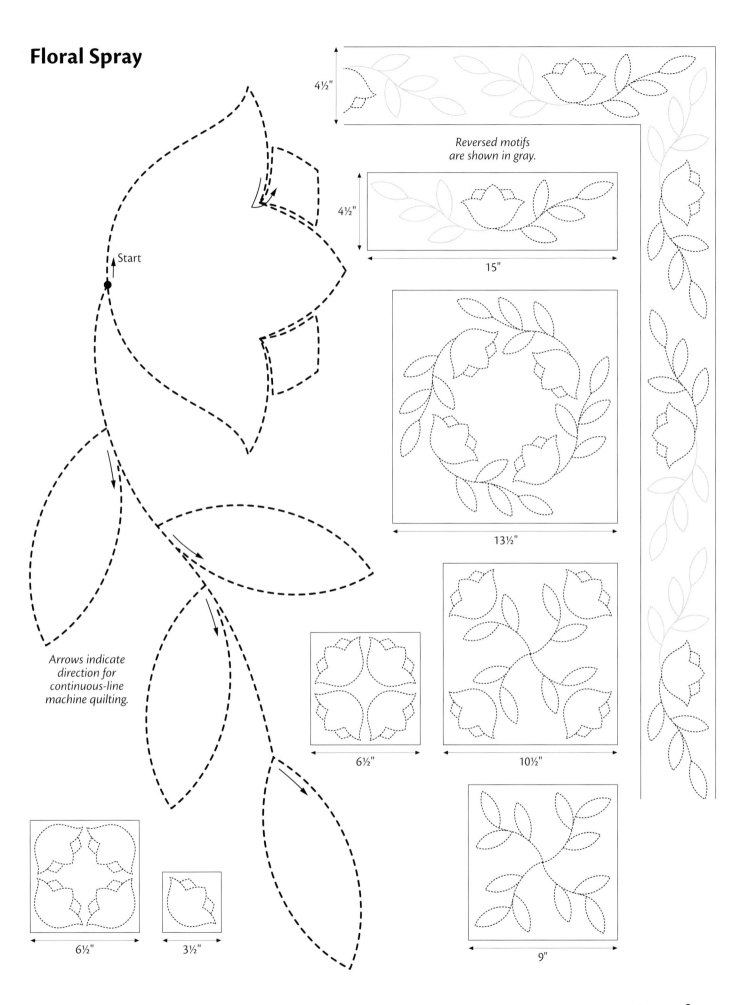

Reversed motifs are shown in gray.

Arrows indicate direction for continuous-line machine quilting.

Start

4½"

4½"

15"

13½"

6½"

10½"

6½"

3½"

9"

Morning's Glory Q

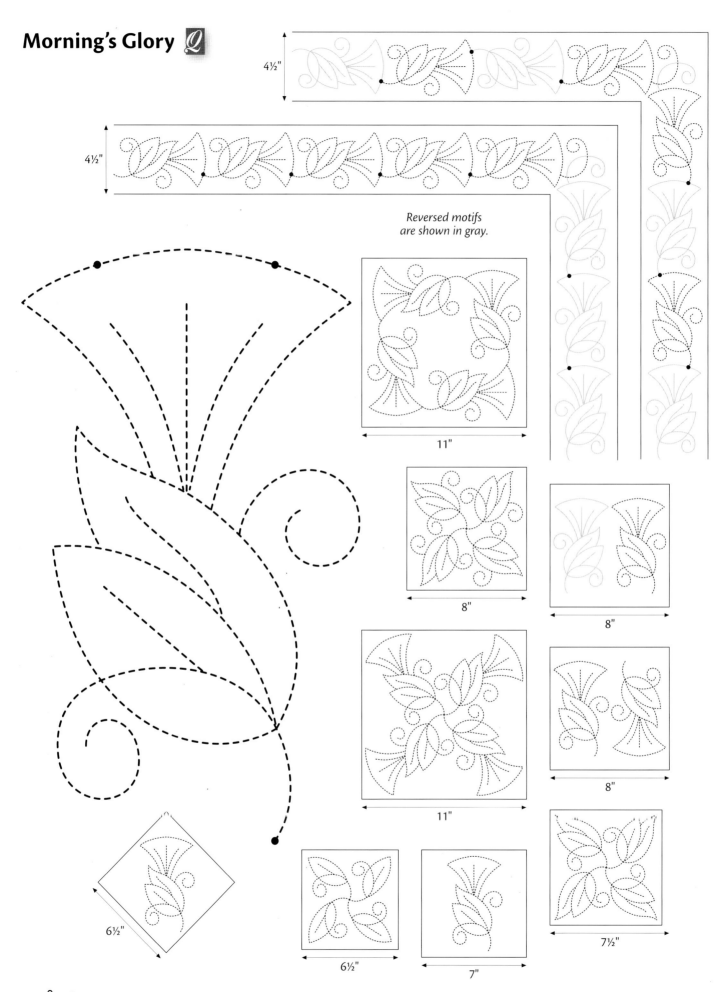

Reversed motifs
are shown in gray.

4½"

4½"

11"

8"

8"

11"

8"

6½"

6½"

7"

7½"

Floral Medley

Arrows indicate direction for continuous-line machine quilting.

Iris Jubilee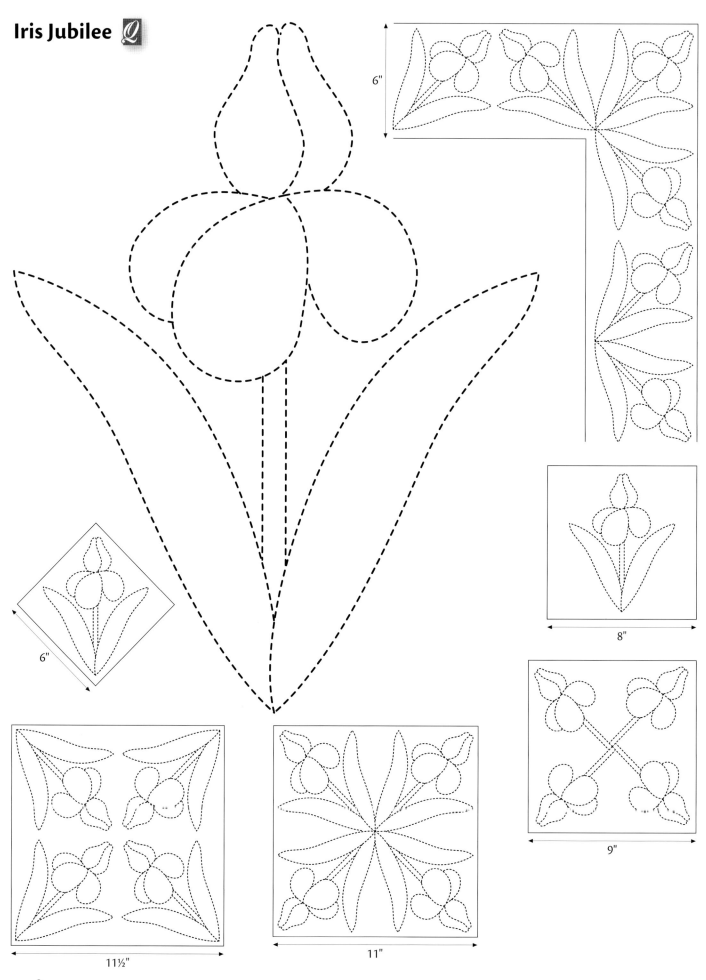

Blossom Vine Q

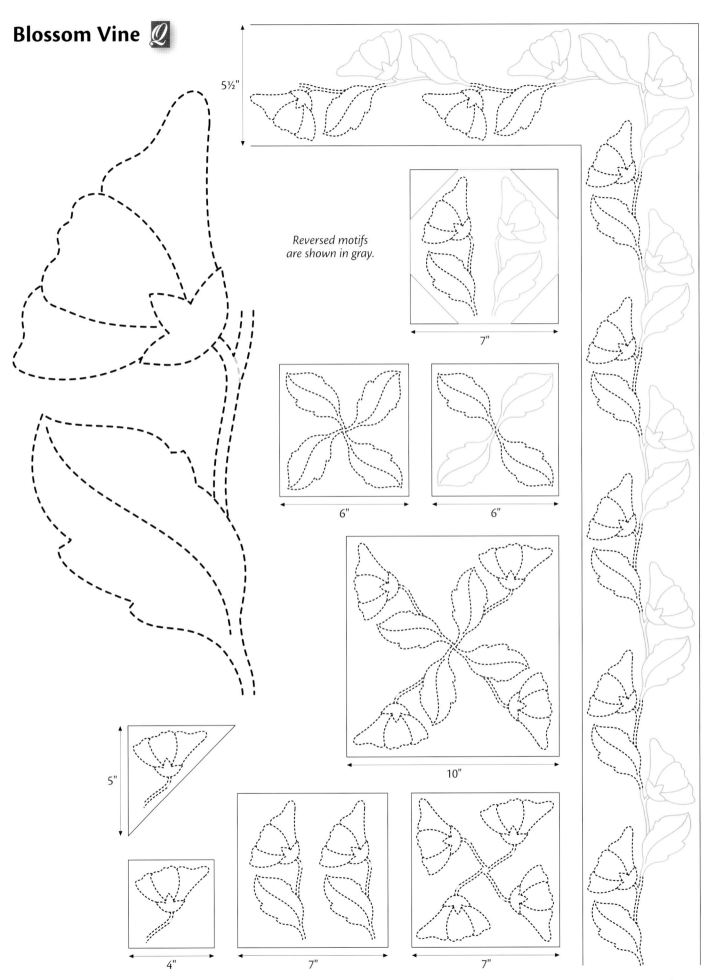

5½"

Reversed motifs are shown in gray.

7"

6"

6"

10"

5"

4"

7"

7"

Daffodil Fancy

Reversed motifs are shown in gray.

5½"

5½"

10"

10"

5½"

8"

5"

2½"

2½"

Rondo

Reversed motifs
are shown in gray.

6"

4"

5½"

7"

7½"

10"

13"

Dandy Daisy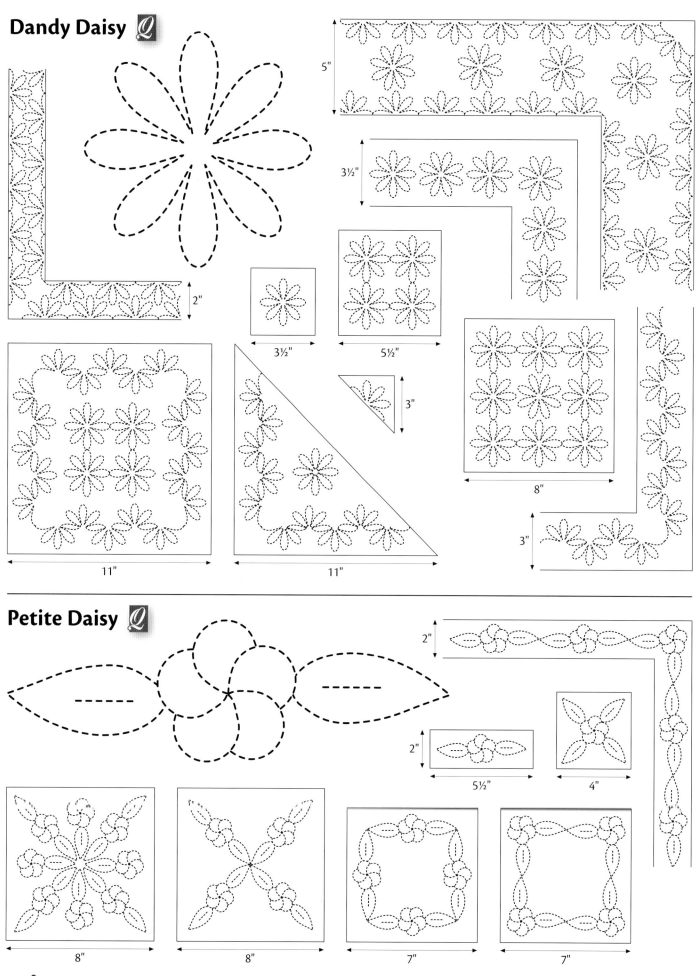

5"

3½"

2"

3½"

5½"

8"

3"

3"

11"

11"

Petite Daisy

2"

2"

5½"

4"

8"

8"

7"

7"

Fanciful Flowers

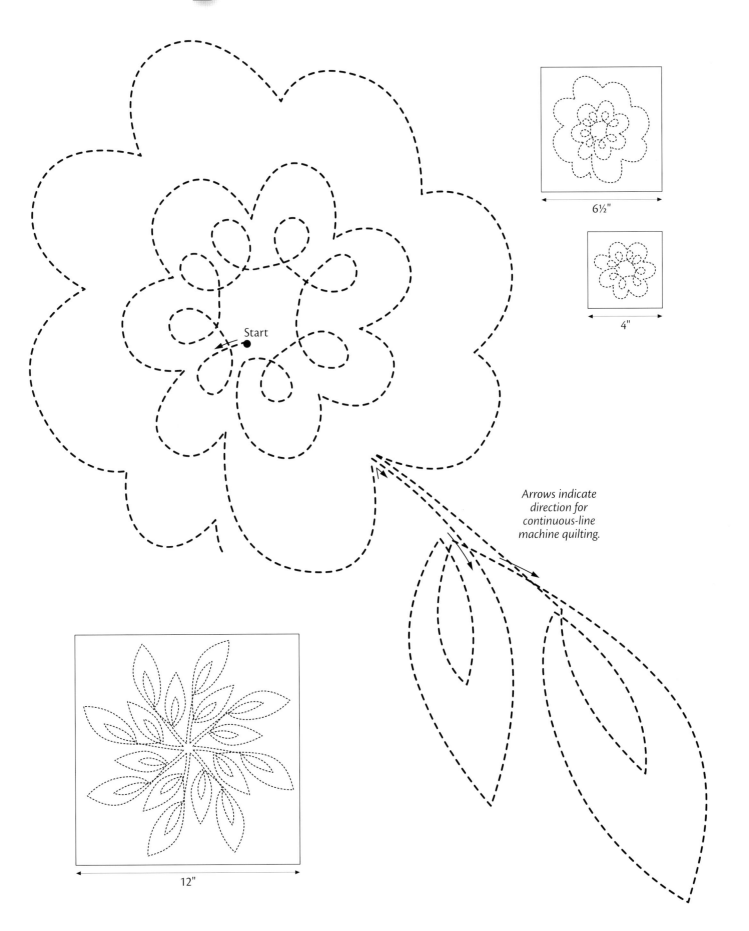

Start

6½"

4"

Arrows indicate
direction for
continuous-line
machine quilting.

12"

Wandering Summer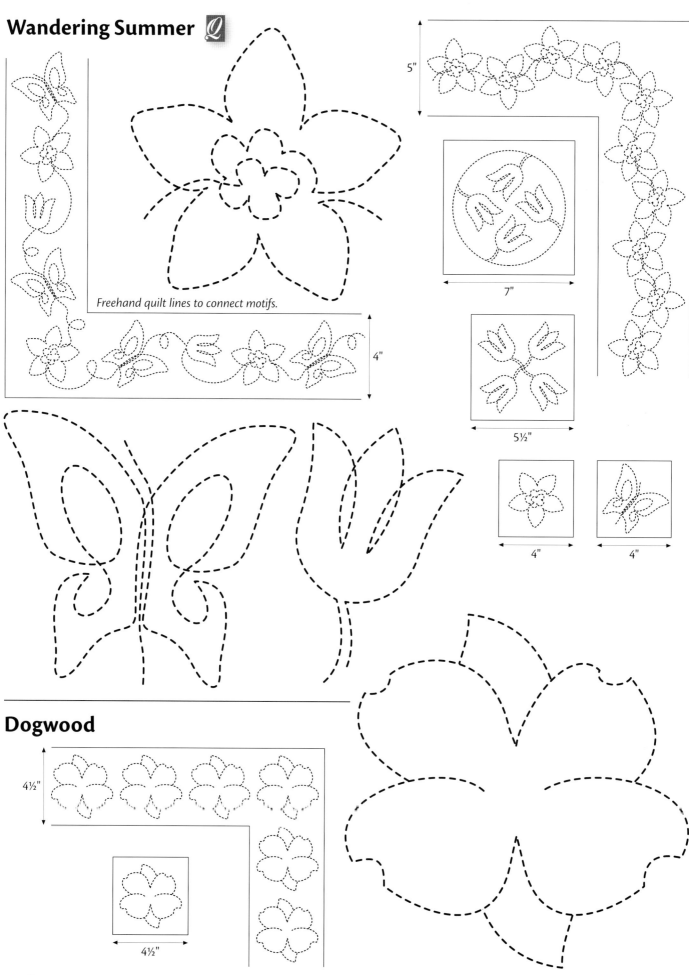

Freehand quilt lines to connect motifs.

5"

7"

4"

5½"

4"

4"

Dogwood

4½"

4½"

Tulip Wreath

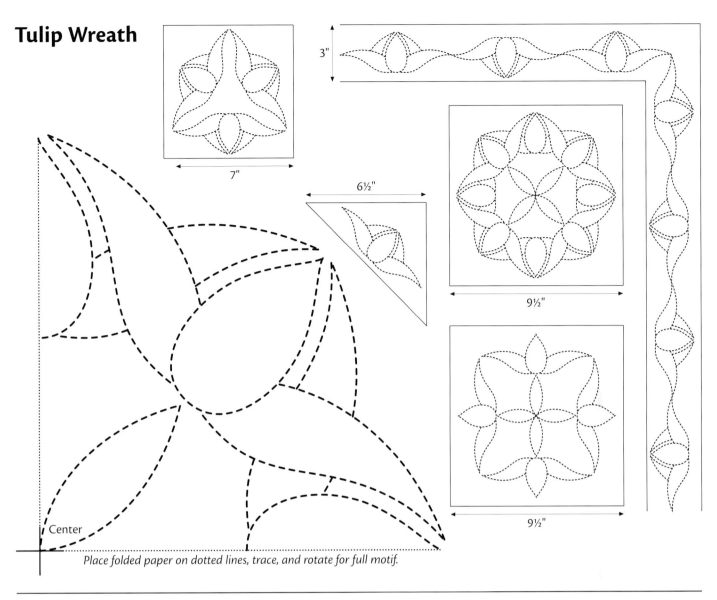

7"

3"

6½"

9½"

9½"

Center

Place folded paper on dotted lines, trace, and rotate for full motif.

Snow Blossom

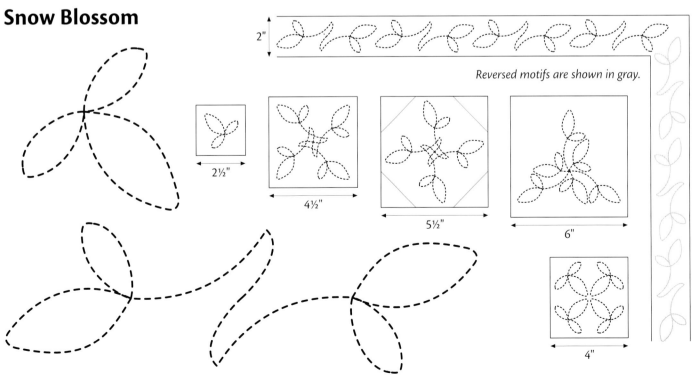

2"

Reversed motifs are shown in gray.

2½"

4½"

5½"

6"

4"

Sundae Surprise Q

8½"

12½"

Place folded paper on dotted lines, trace, and rotate for full motif.

Center

12"

12"

10"

Butterfly Garden

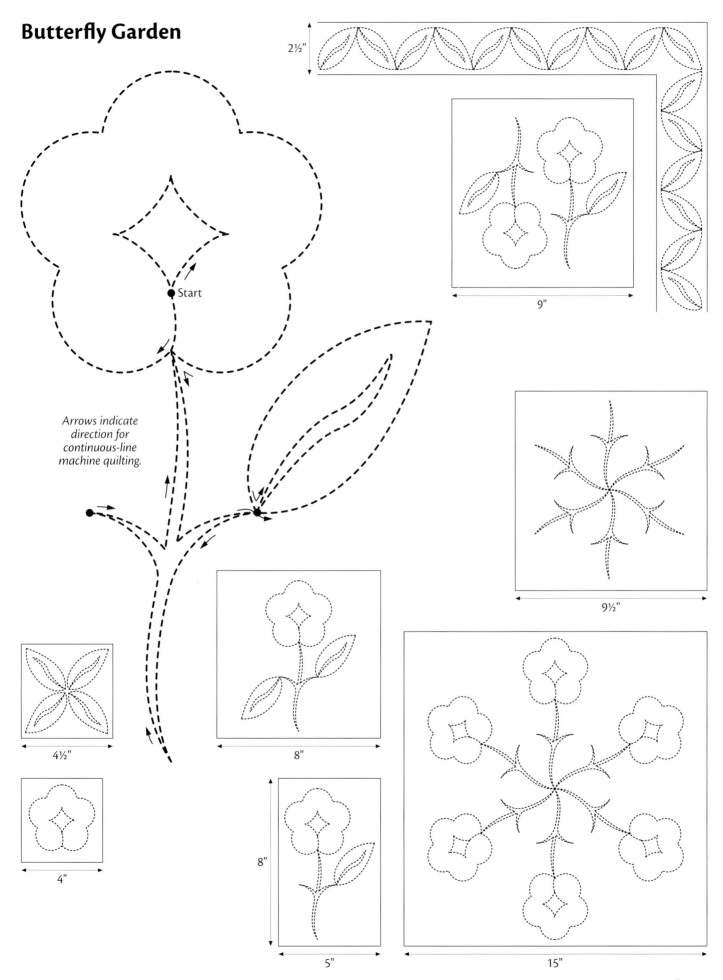

● Start

Arrows indicate direction for continuous-line machine quilting.

2½"

9"

9½"

4½"

4"

8"

8"

5"

15"

Sunflower

6"

6"

3½"

8"

3"

6"

6"

8½"

Climbing Vine

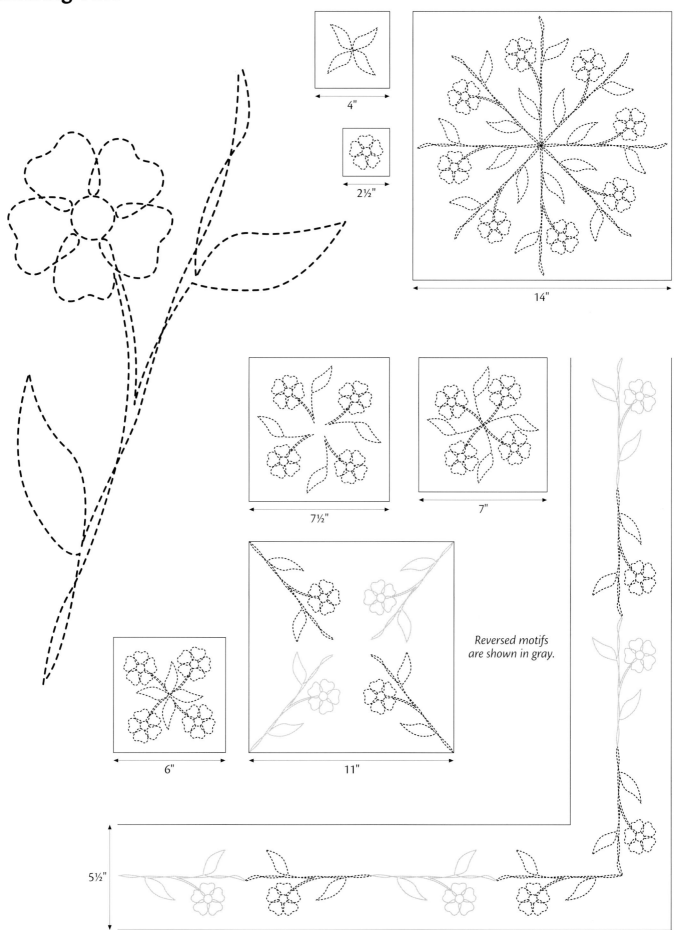

4"

2½"

14"

7½"

7"

*Reversed motifs
are shown in gray.*

6"

11"

5½"

Glorious Morning

2½"

5"

5"

3½"

3½"

7"

4"

8½"

Wandering Flower

10½"

13"

Tulip

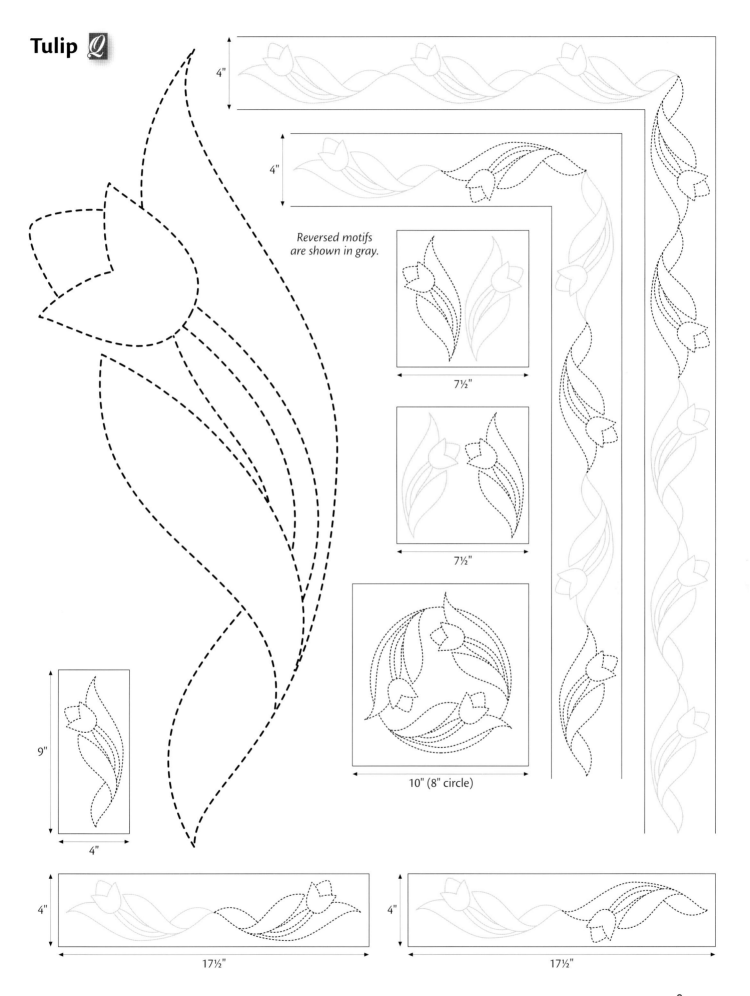

Reversed motifs
are shown in gray.

4"

4"

7½"

7½"

10" (8" circle)

9"

4"

4"

17½"

4"

17½"

Garden Party

6½"

3"

6"

3"

4½"

15"

15"

3"

4"

4"

2½"

3"

12"

9"

Foods

Teacher's Pet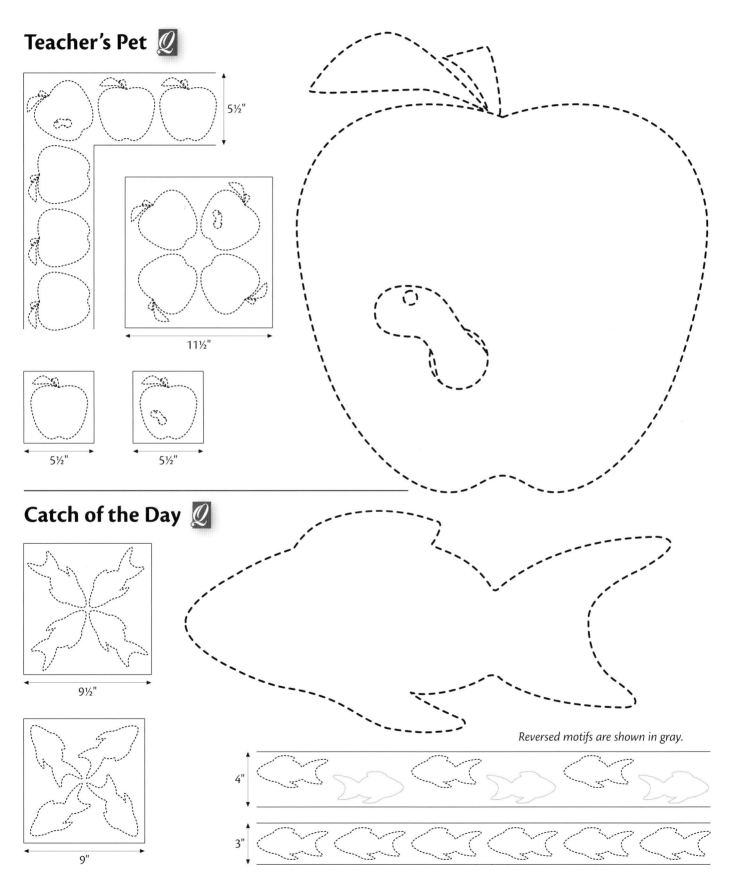

5½"

11½"

5½"   5½"

Catch of the Day

9½"

9"

Reversed motifs are shown in gray.

4"

3"

Ravishing Radishes

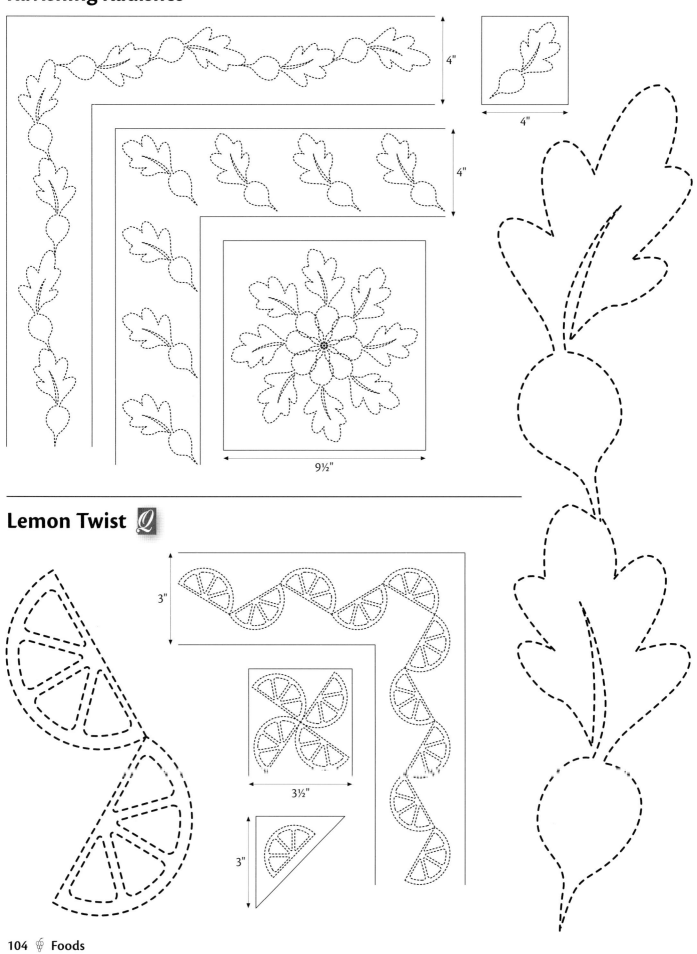

4"

4"

9½"

4"

Lemon Twist Q

3"

3½"

3"

Berry Blossom

Peach Harvest

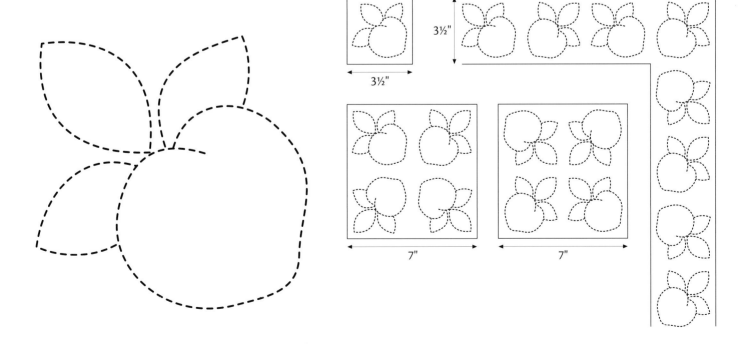

Herbal Medley

3½"

3½"   3½"

3½"

5"

5½"   8½"

5"

5"   5"

6"

8"

Granny Smith's

3"

2½"

12"

5"

6½"

7½"

7½"

Bite o' Melon

3½"

4½"

6"

6"

Strawberry Fields

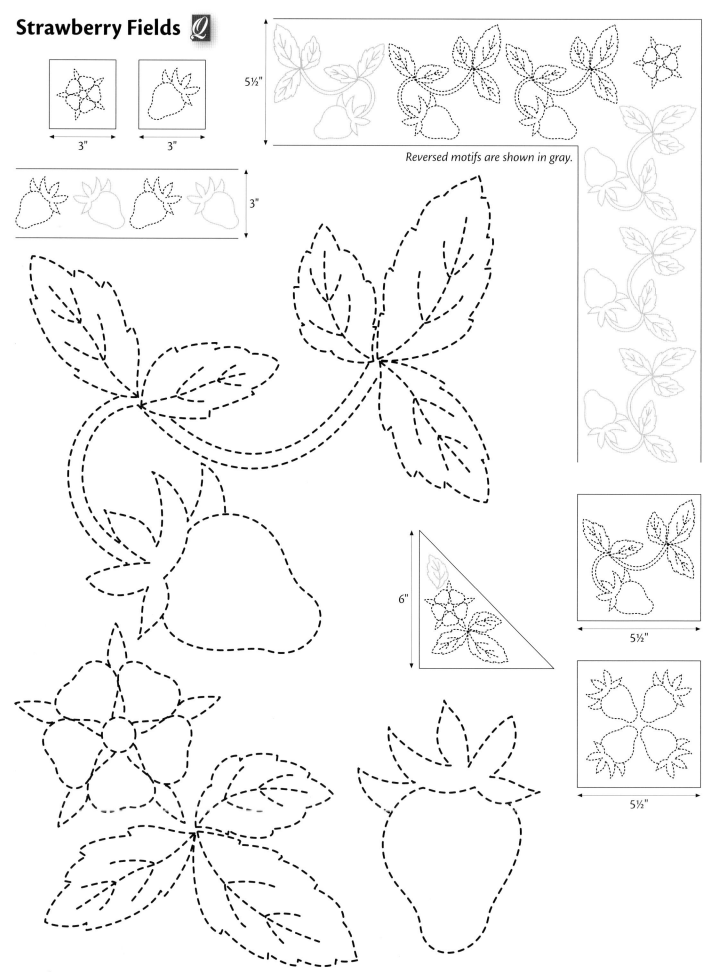

Reversed motifs are shown in gray.

5½"

3"

3"

3"

6"

5½"

5½"

Cherry

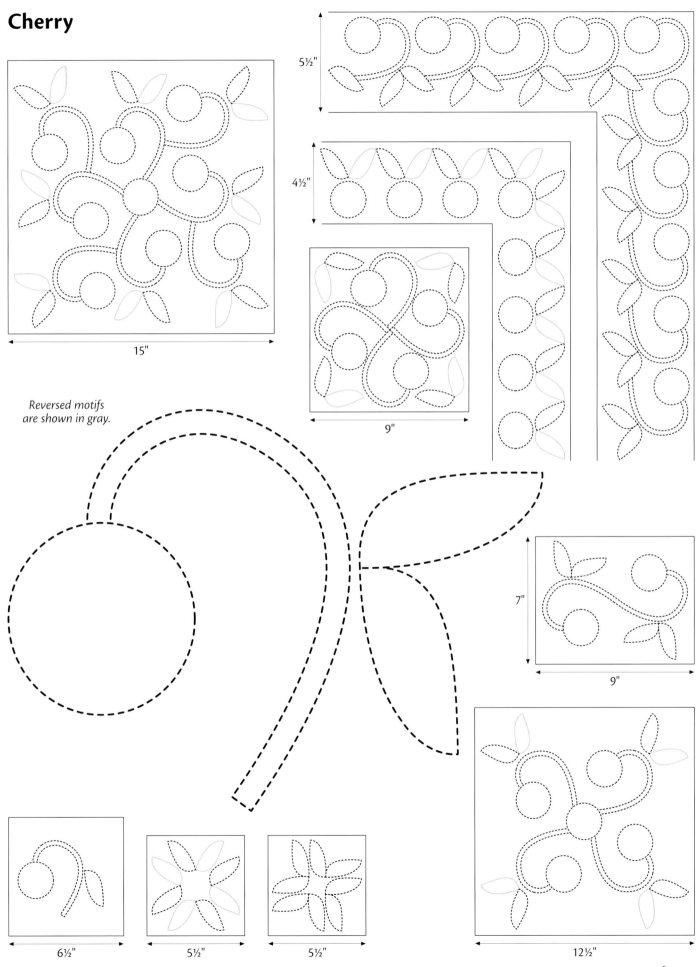

15"

5½"

4½"

9"

Reversed motifs are shown in gray.

7"

9"

6½"

5½"

5½"

12½"

Geometric Shapes

Rippling Waves

4½"

8"

Dancing Curls

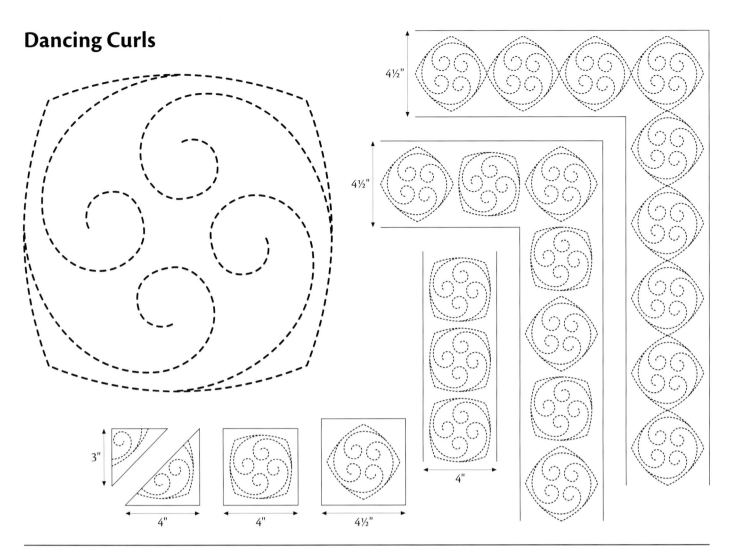

Wavelet

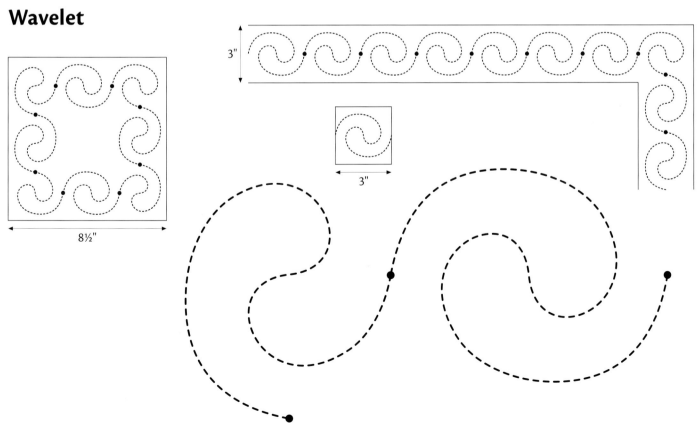

Whirlabout

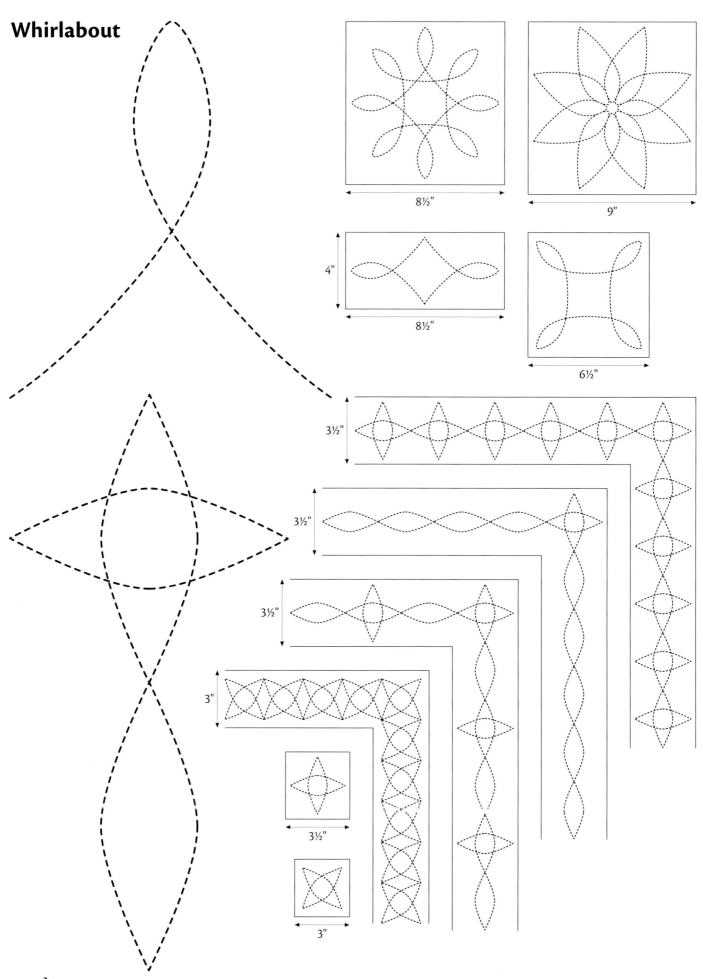

Candle Flame

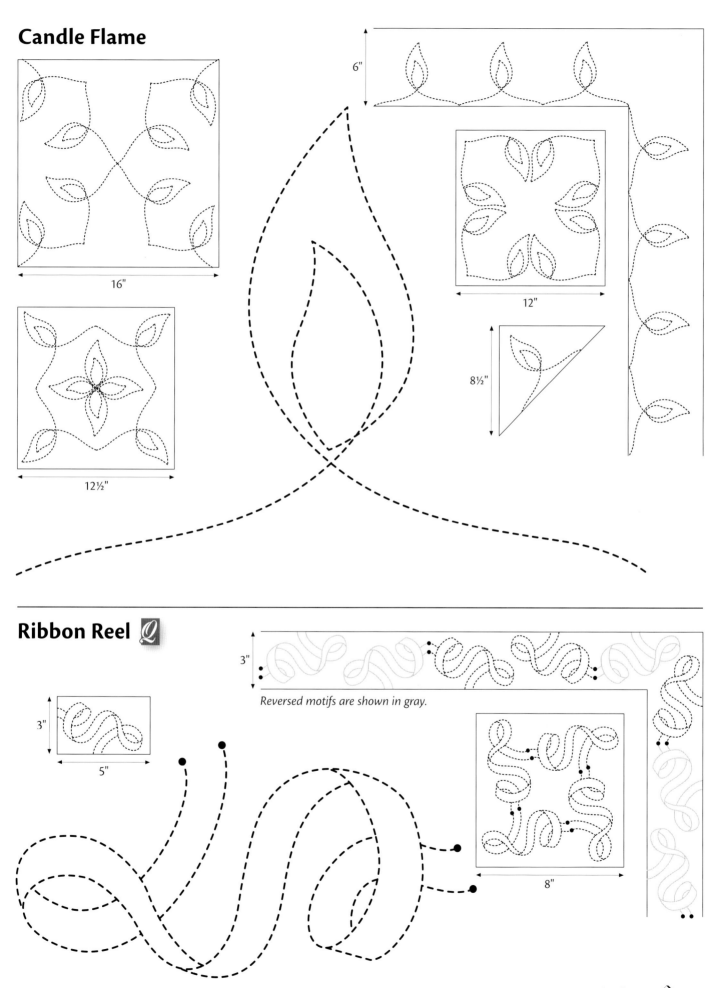

16"

12½"

6"

12"

8½"

Ribbon Reel

3"

Reversed motifs are shown in gray.

3"

5"

8"

Autumn Breeze

Reversed motifs
are shown in gray.

3½"

8½"

5½"

Celebration 2

Reversed motifs
are shown in gray.

9"

11"

13"

12"

3½"

Yukon Cable

Partial motifs
are shown in gray.

4"

4"

3"

3"

2½"

2½"

2½"

12½"

7½"

10"

4"

3"

Ribbon Dance

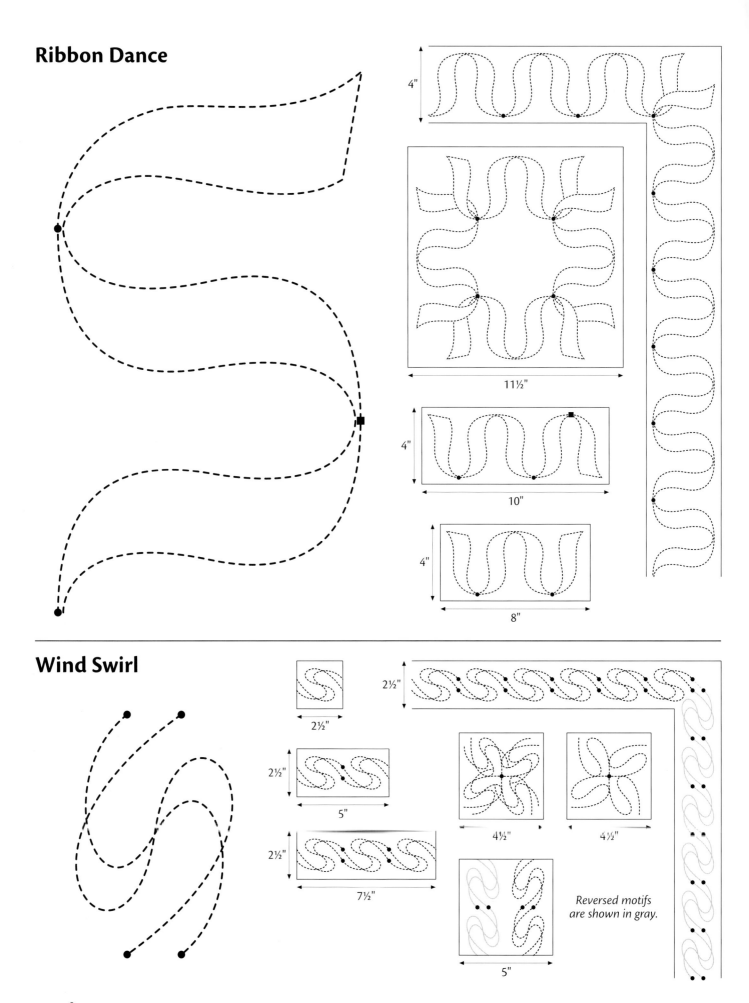

Wind Swirl

4"

11½"

4"

10"

4"

8"

2½"

2½"

2½"

2½"

5"

7½"

4½"

4½"

5"

Reversed motifs are shown in gray.

Furrow Cable

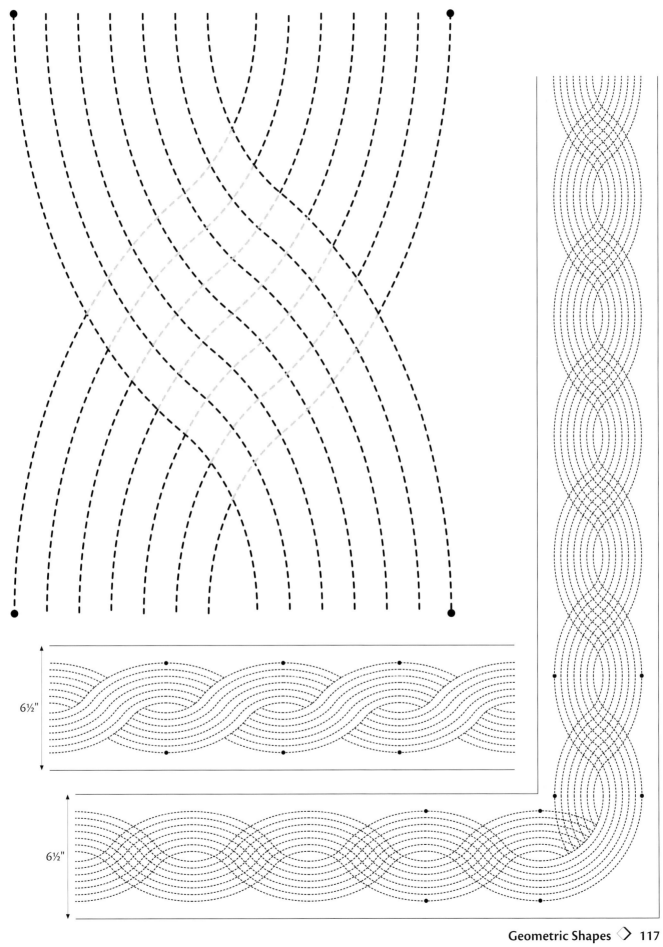

6½"

6½"

Fish Splash

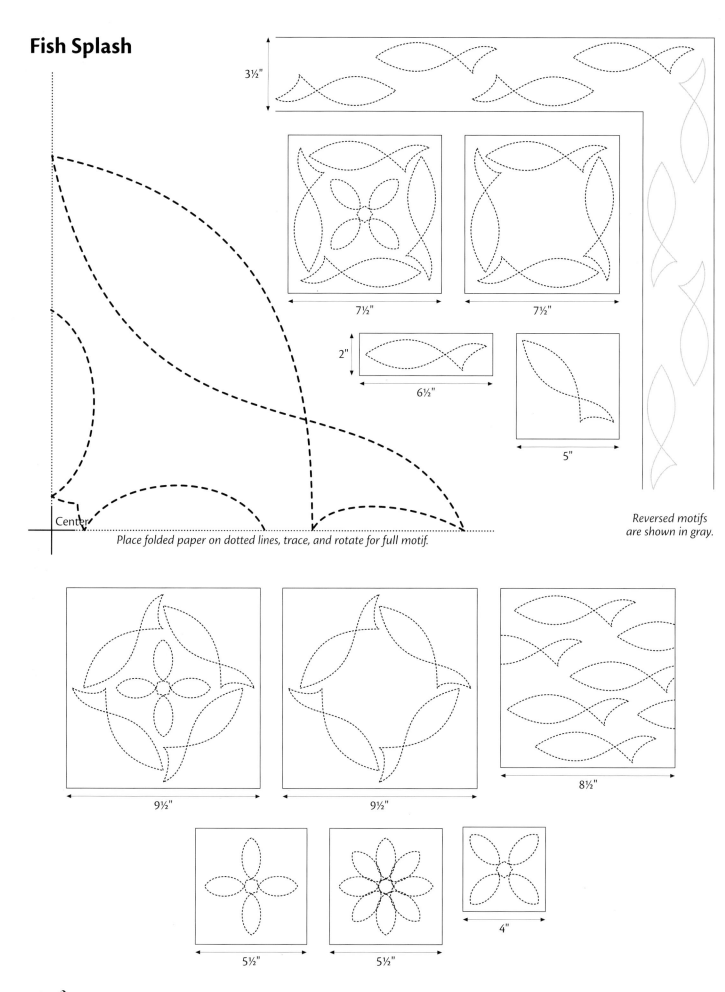

3½"

7½"

7½"

2"

6½"

5"

*Reversed motifs
are shown in gray.*

Center

Place folded paper on dotted lines, trace, and rotate for full motif.

9½"

9½"

8½"

5½"

5½"

4"

Celtic Knot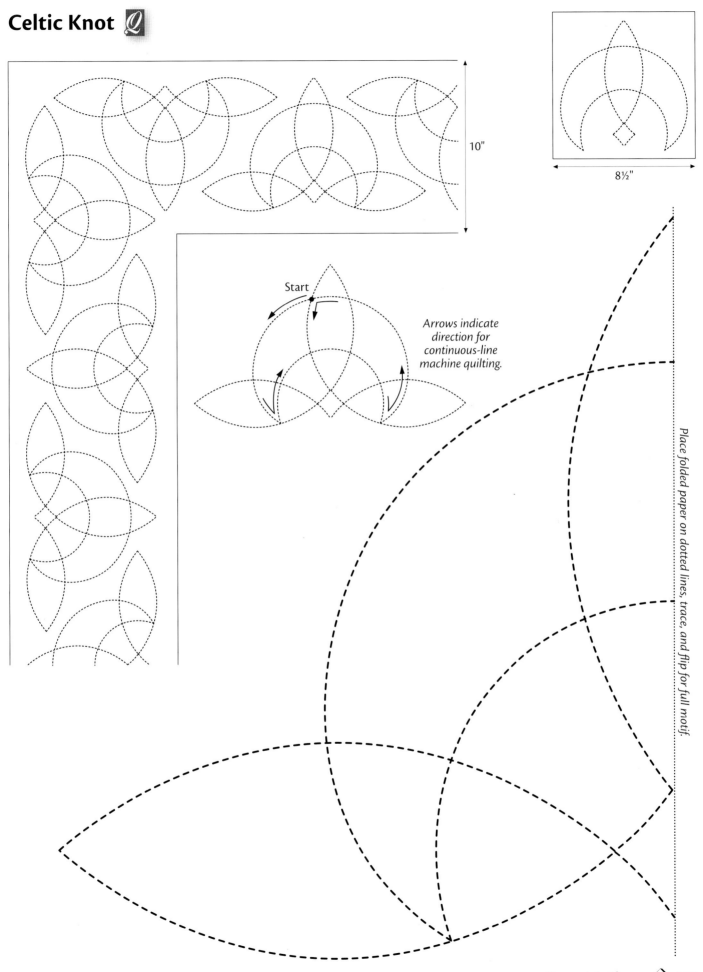

10"

8½"

Start

Arrows indicate direction for continuous-line machine quilting.

Place folded paper on dotted lines, trace, and flip for full motif.

Arrowhead

3½"

2"

10½"

6"

7"

9½"

10½"

Celestial

3½"

3½"

5"

3½"

8"

6"

6"

8"

Celtic Chain

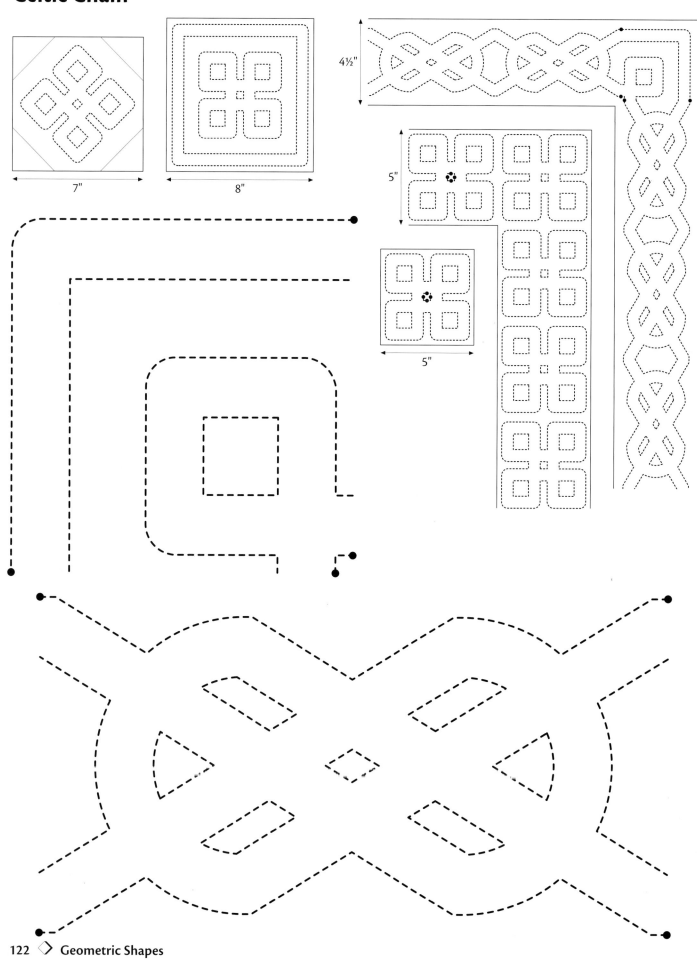

7"

8"

4½"

5"

5"

Golf Ball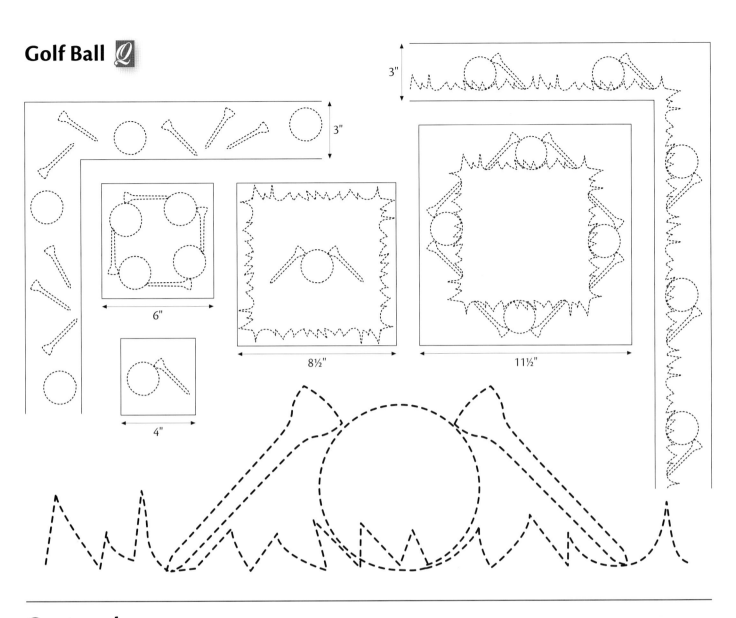

3"

6"

8½"

11½"

4"

Guatemala

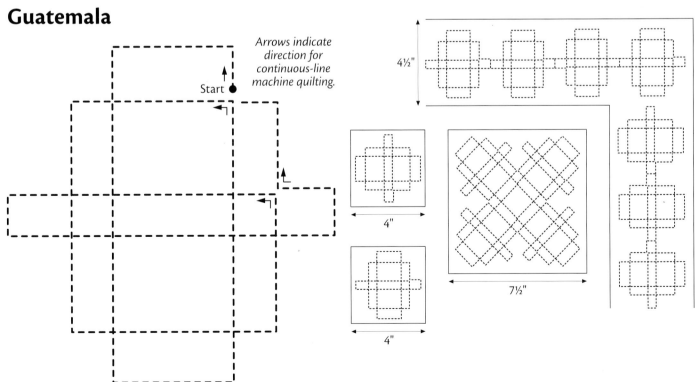

Arrows indicate direction for continuous-line machine quilting.

Start

4½"

4"

4"

7½"

Loops and Swirls

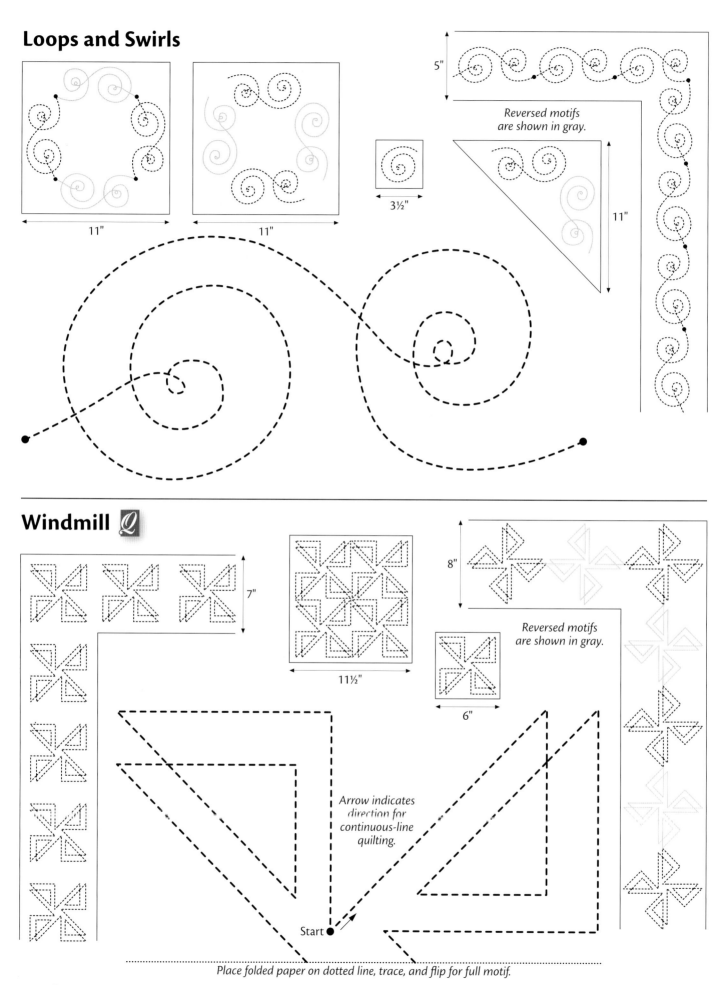

11"

11"

3½"

5"

11"

Reversed motifs are shown in gray.

Windmill Q

7"

11½"

6"

8"

Reversed motifs are shown in gray.

Arrow indicates direction for continuous-line quilting.

Start

Place folded paper on dotted line, trace, and flip for full motif.

Spirals and Scrolls

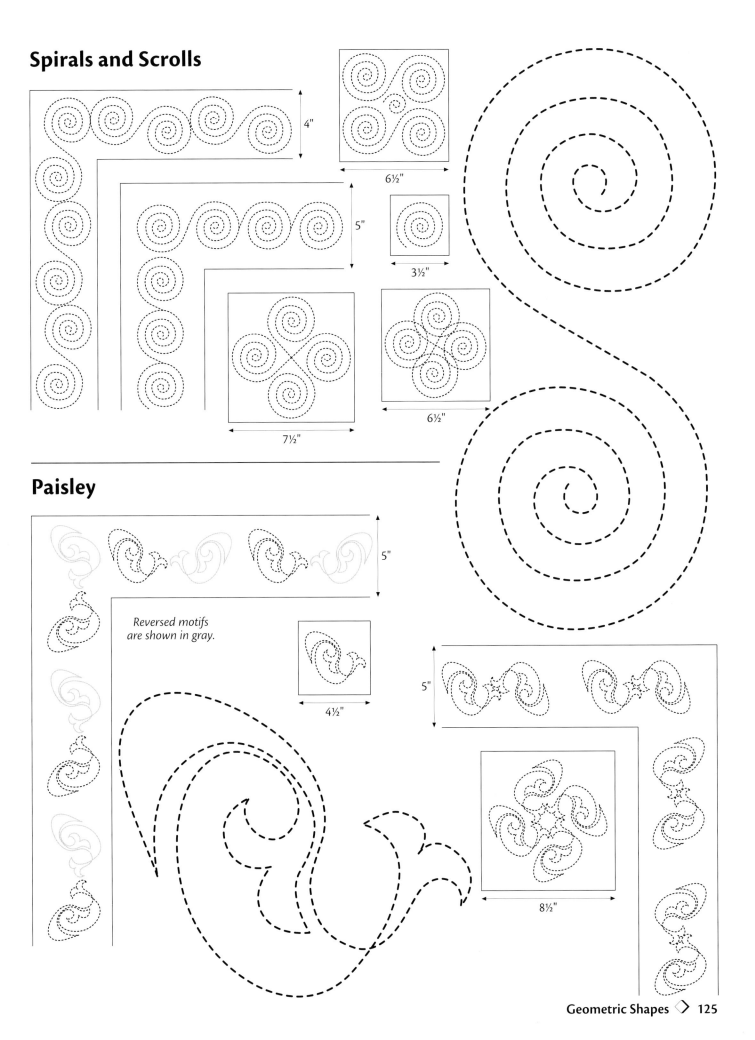

4"

6½"

5"

3½"

7½"

6½"

Paisley

5"

*Reversed motifs
are shown in gray.*

4½"

5"

8½"

Diamond

3½"

5"

3"

4"

8"

3"

7"

5½"

Whirlybows

10"

9½"

Freehand quilt lines to connect the motifs.

Center

Place folded paper on dotted lines, trace, and rotate for full motif.

Hanover

11½"

4"

4"

4"

4"

5½"

5"

2"

4"

2"

9½"

5"

11"

4"

10"

10"

Cable Border

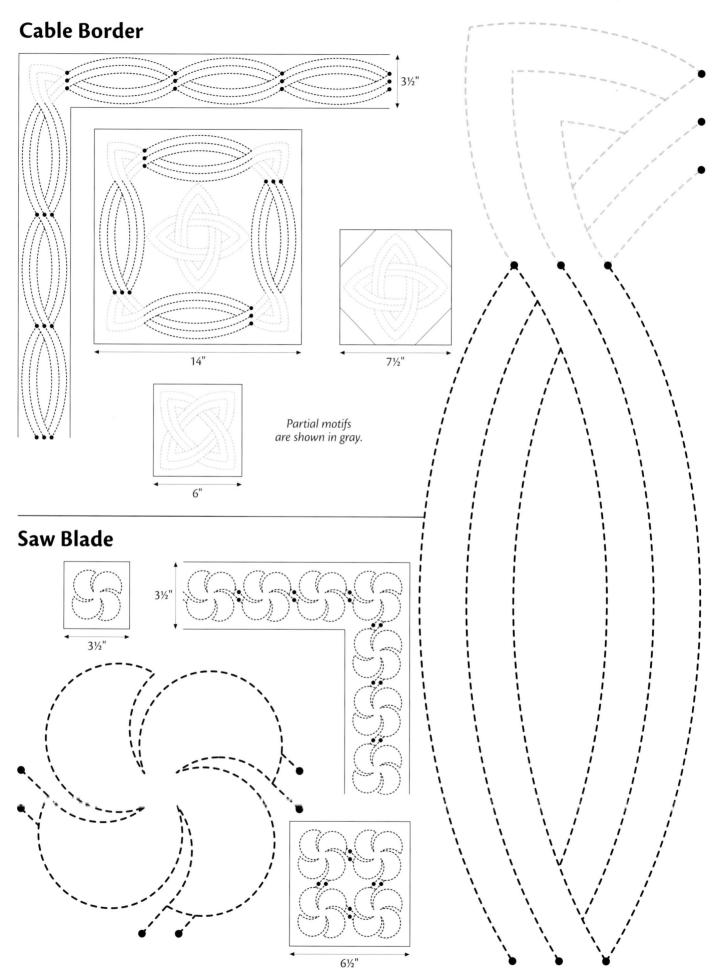

3½"

14"

7½"

6"

*Partial motifs
are shown in gray.*

Saw Blade

3½"

3½"

3½"

6½"

Shadowbox

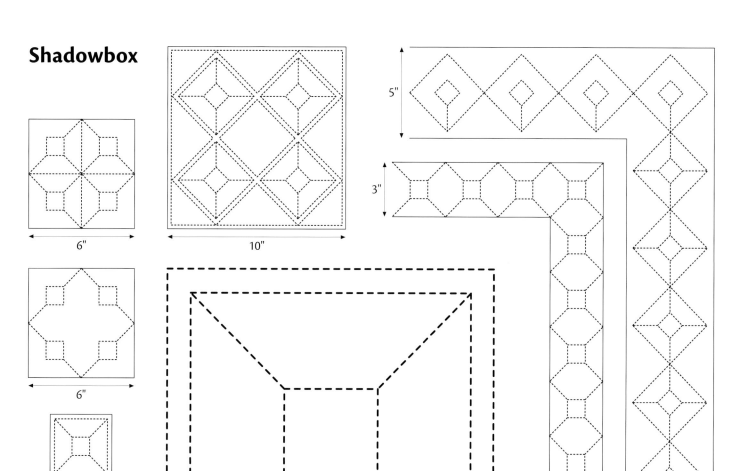

6"

10"

5"

3"

6"

3½"

Star in the Window

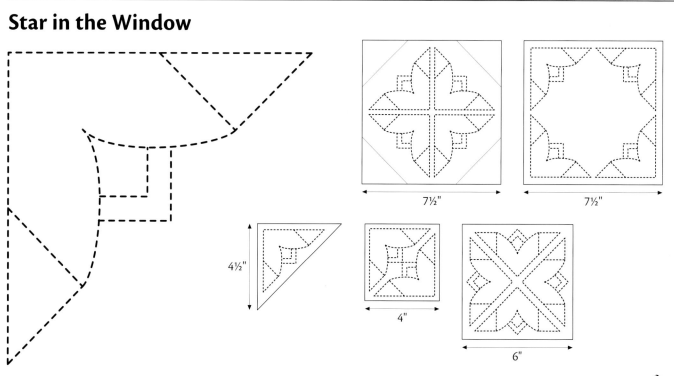

7½"

7½"

4½"

4"

6"

Lattice Blossom

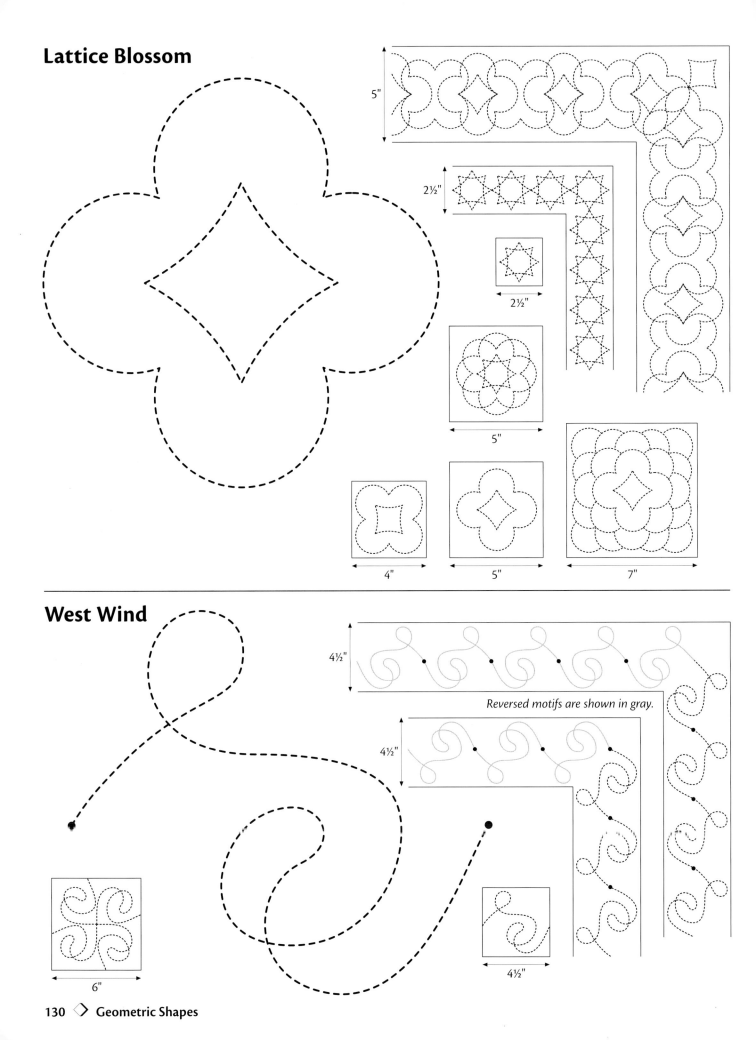

Reversed motifs are shown in gray.

West Wind

Explorers

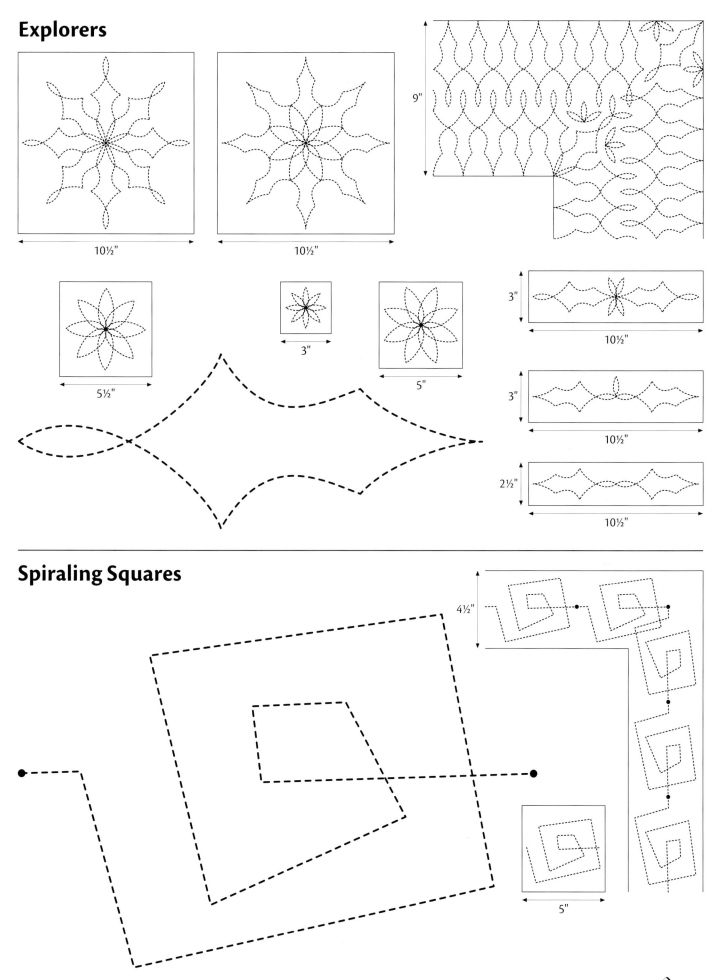

10½"

10½"

9"

5½"

3"

5"

3"

10½"

3"

10½"

2½"

10½"

Spiraling Squares

4½"

5"

Twirl Around

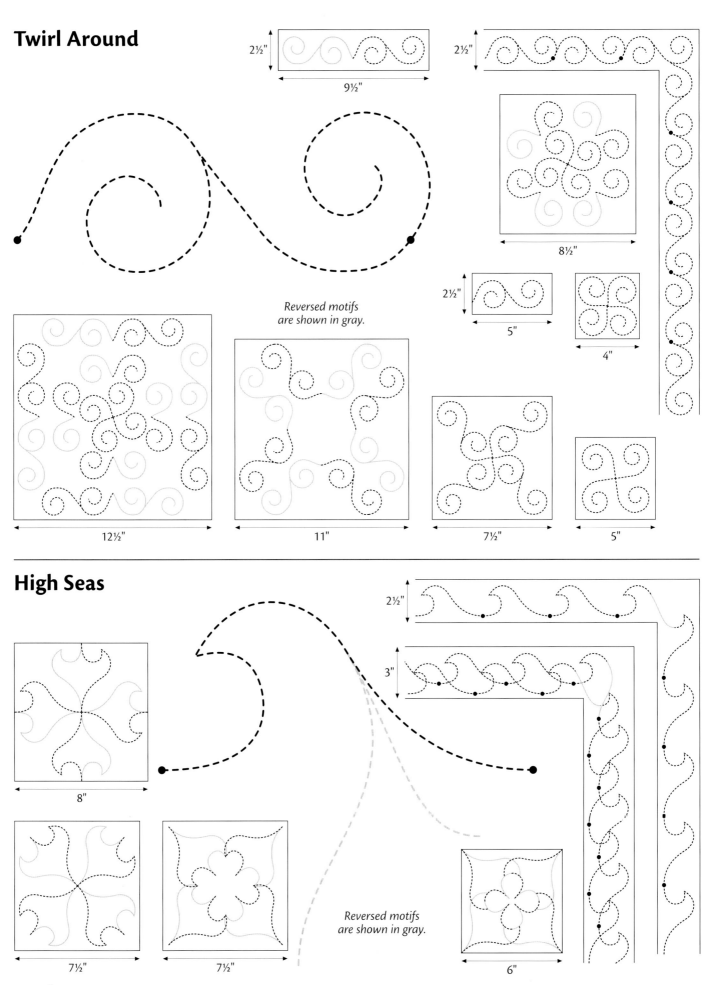

Reversed motifs
are shown in gray.

2½"

9½"

2½"

8½"

2½"

5"

4"

12½"

11"

7½"

5"

High Seas

2½"

3"

8"

7½"

7½"

6"

Reversed motifs
are shown in gray.

Today's Touch

Whirligig

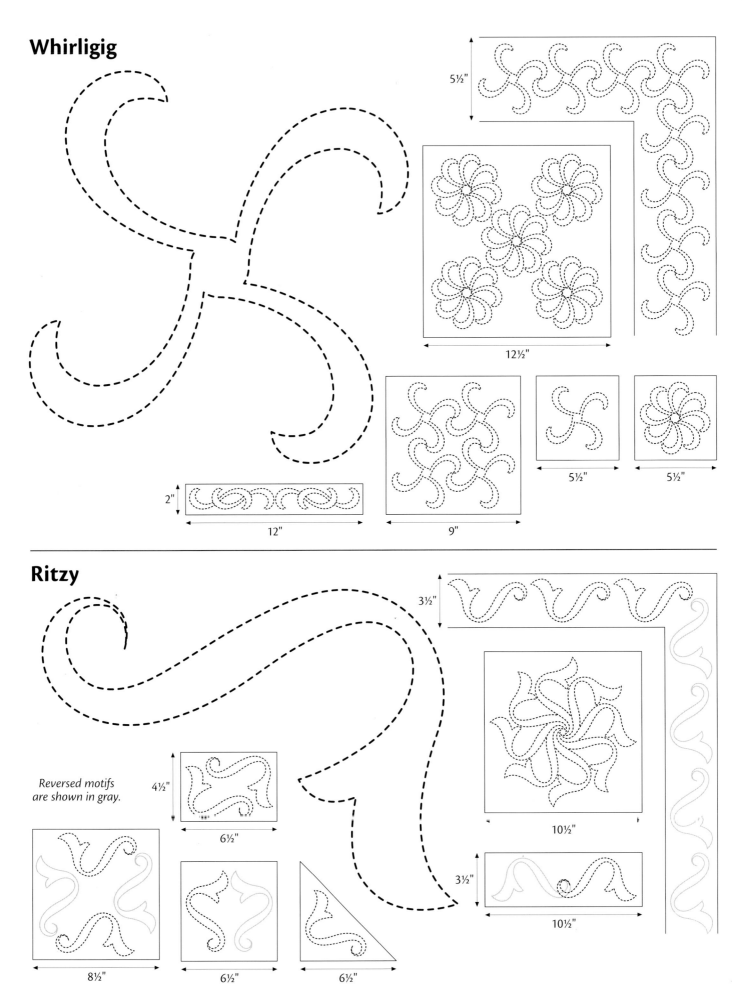

5½"

12½"

2"

12"

9"

5½"

5½"

Ritzy

3½"

Reversed motifs are shown in gray.

4½"

6½"

10½"

3½"

10½"

8½"

6½"

6½"

Fleur-de-Lis

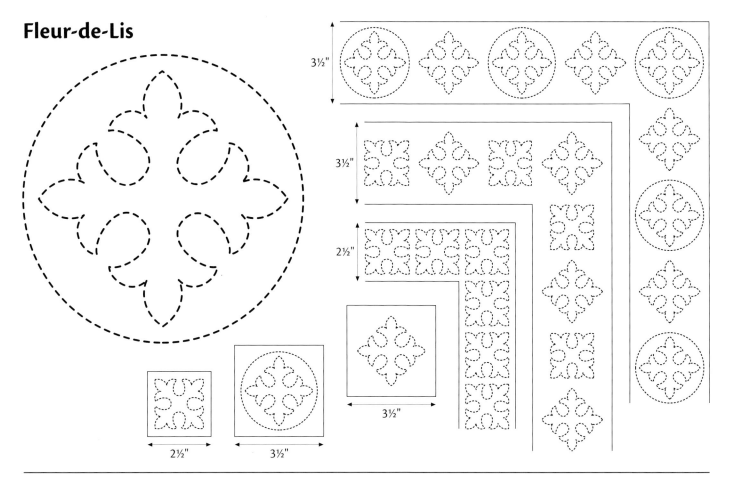

3½"

3½"

2½"

2½"

3½"

3½"

3½"

Gibraltar

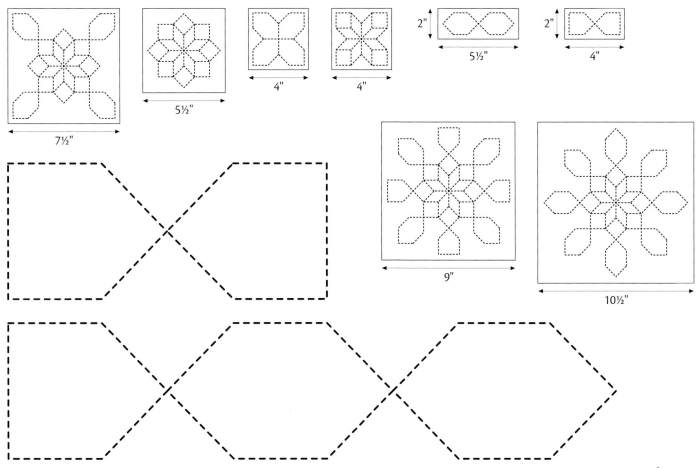

7½"

5½"

4"

4"

2"
5½"

2"
4"

9"

10½"

Lemon Peel

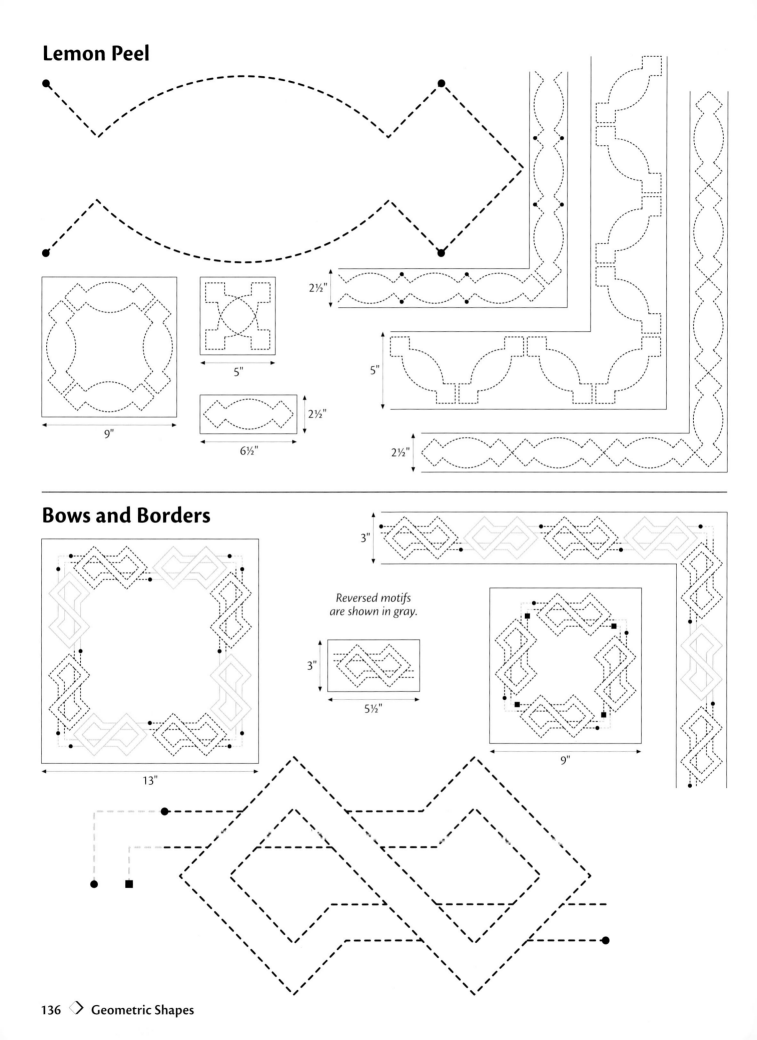

9"

5"

2½"

6½"

2½"

5"

2½"

Bows and Borders

3"

Reversed motifs are shown in gray.

3"

5½"

9"

13"

9"

Between Times

Reversed motifs are shown in gray.

3½"

3½"

3"

5"

6½"

Twirly Tucks

Reversed motifs are shown in gray.

4½"

4"

4"

8½"

8½"

4½"

Swirl

6"

6"

4½"

4½"

Palace Steps Q

6½"

3½"

3½"

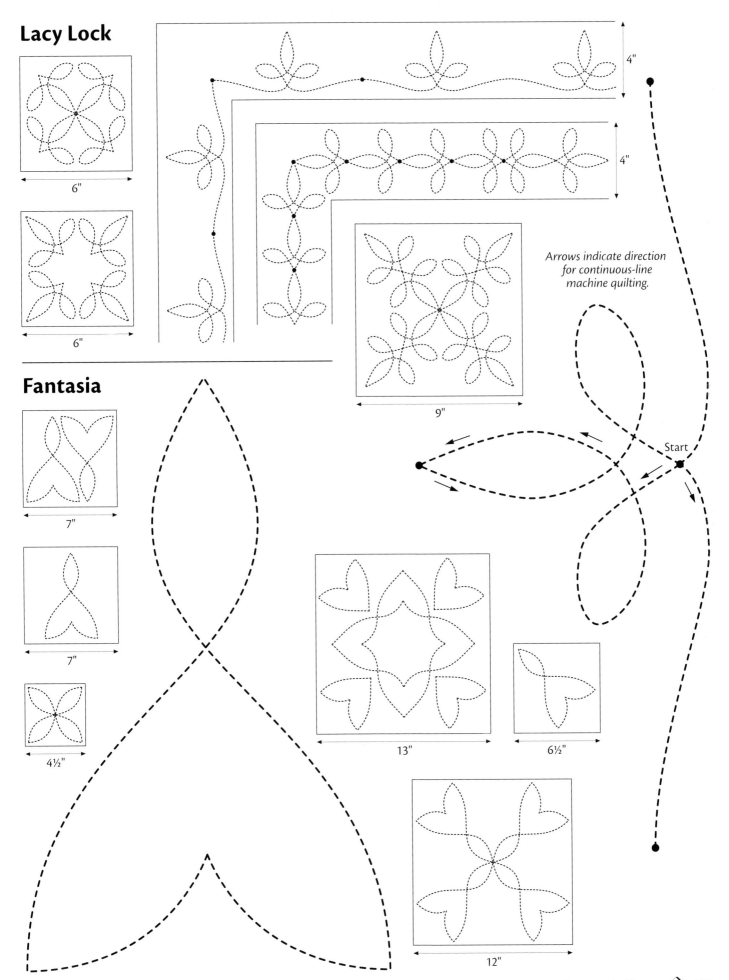

Lacy Lock

6"

6"

4"

4"

9"

Arrows indicate direction for continuous-line machine quilting.

Start

Fantasia

7"

7"

4½"

13"

6½"

12"

Starblossom

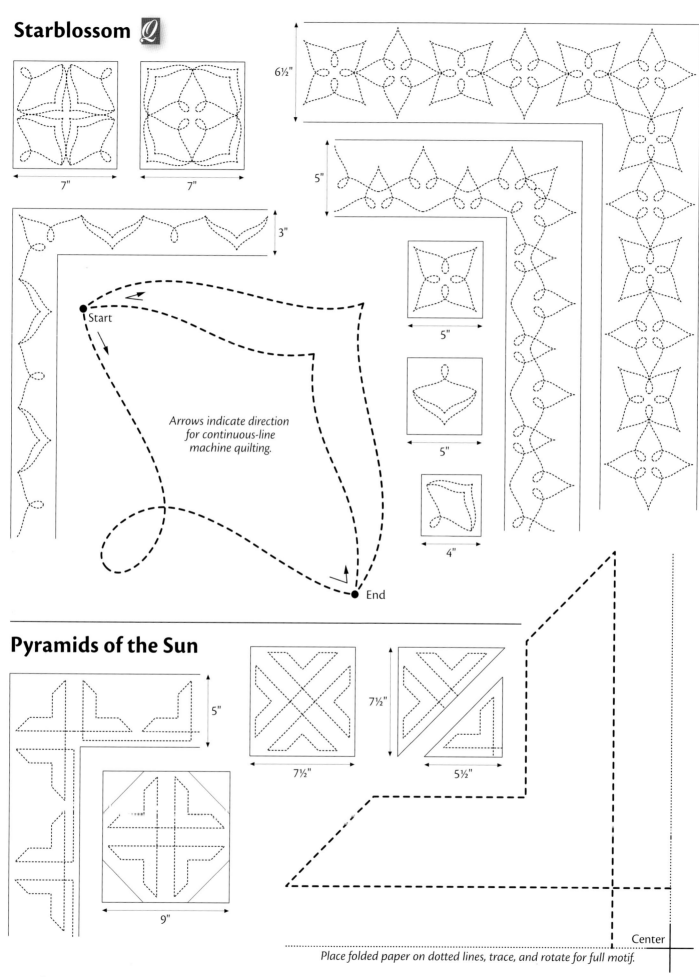

Arrows indicate direction for continuous-line machine quilting.

6½"

5"

3"

7"

7"

5"

5"

4"

Start

End

Pyramids of the Sun

5"

7½"

7½"

5½"

9"

7½"

Center

Place folded paper on dotted lines, trace, and rotate for full motif.

Graceful

5½"

8"

5"

6"

4½"

Win Again

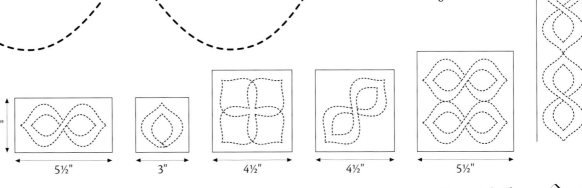

3"

8"

3"

5½"

3"

4½"

4½"

5½"

Irish Cable

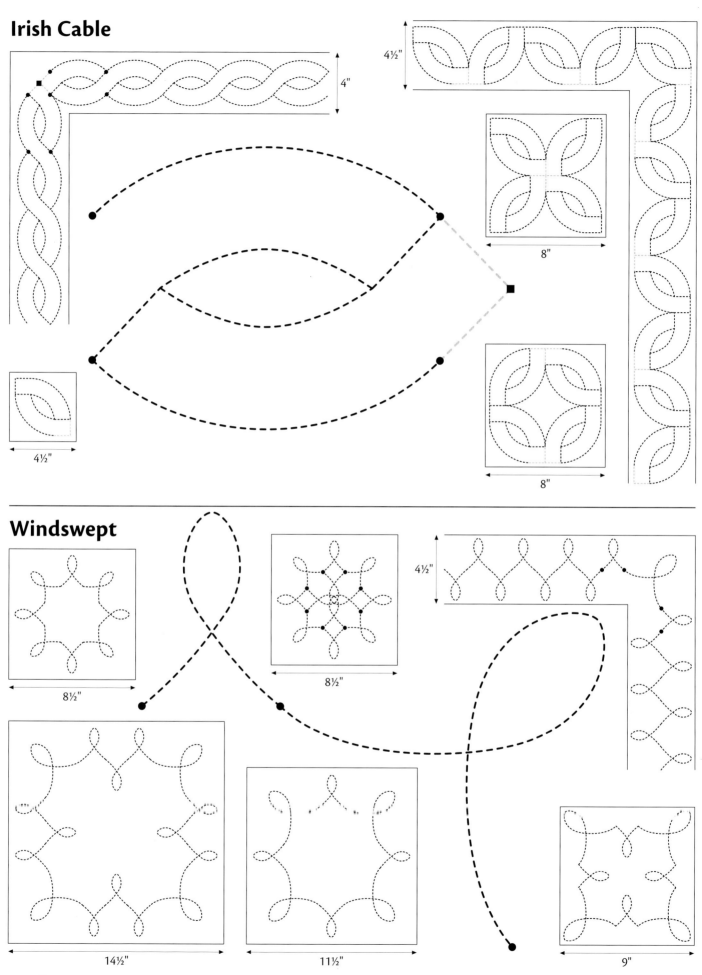

4"

4½"

8"

8"

4½"

Windswept

8½"

8½"

4½"

14½"

11½"

9"

Main Street

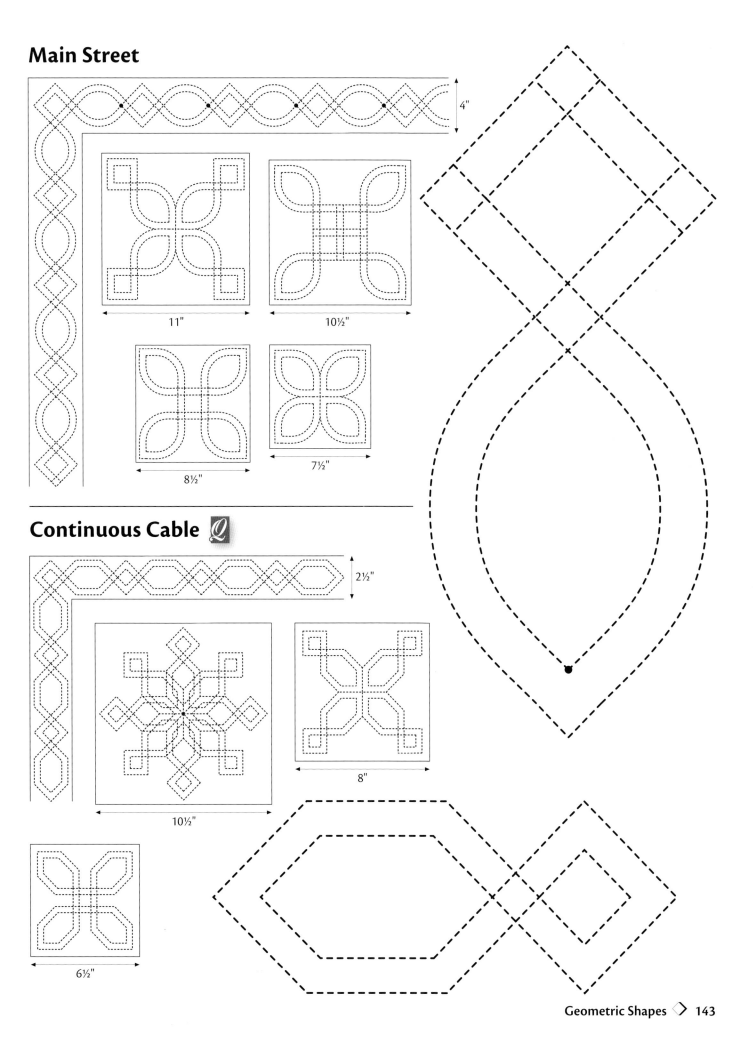

11"

10½"

8½"

7½"

4"

Continuous Cable

2½"

10½"

8"

6½"

Chinook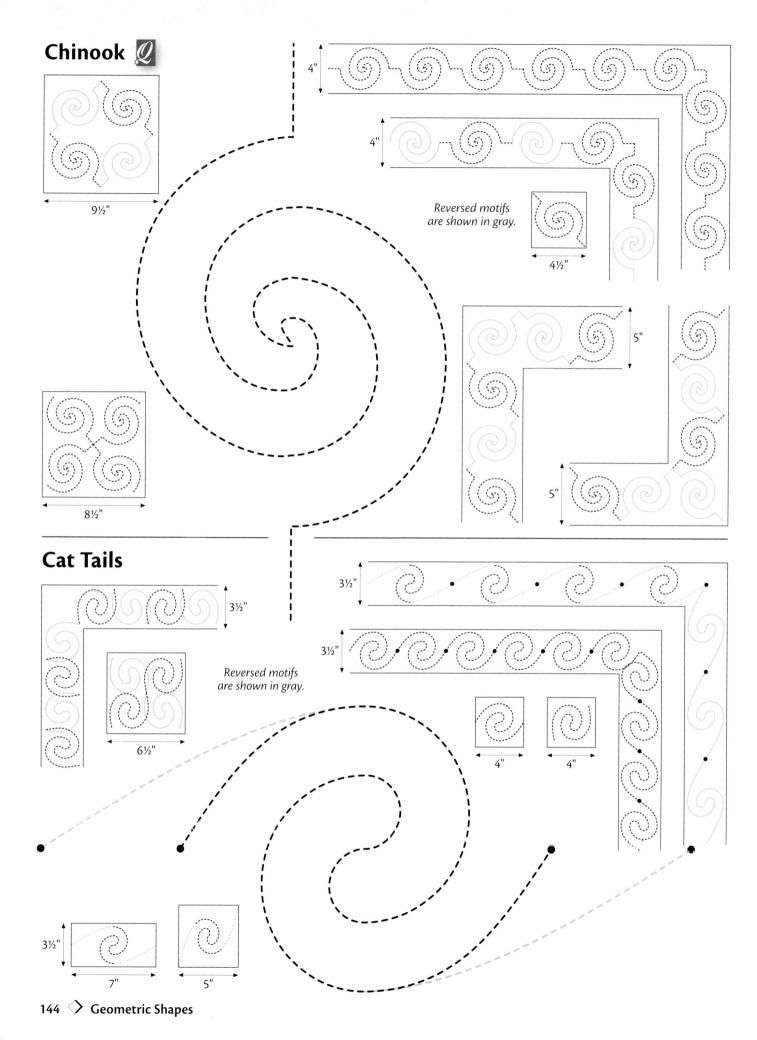

9½"

8½"

Reversed motifs are shown in gray.

4"

4"

4½"

5"

5"

Cat Tails

3½"

6½"

Reversed motifs are shown in gray.

3½"

3½"

4"

4"

3½"

7

5

Hearts

Kissing Hearts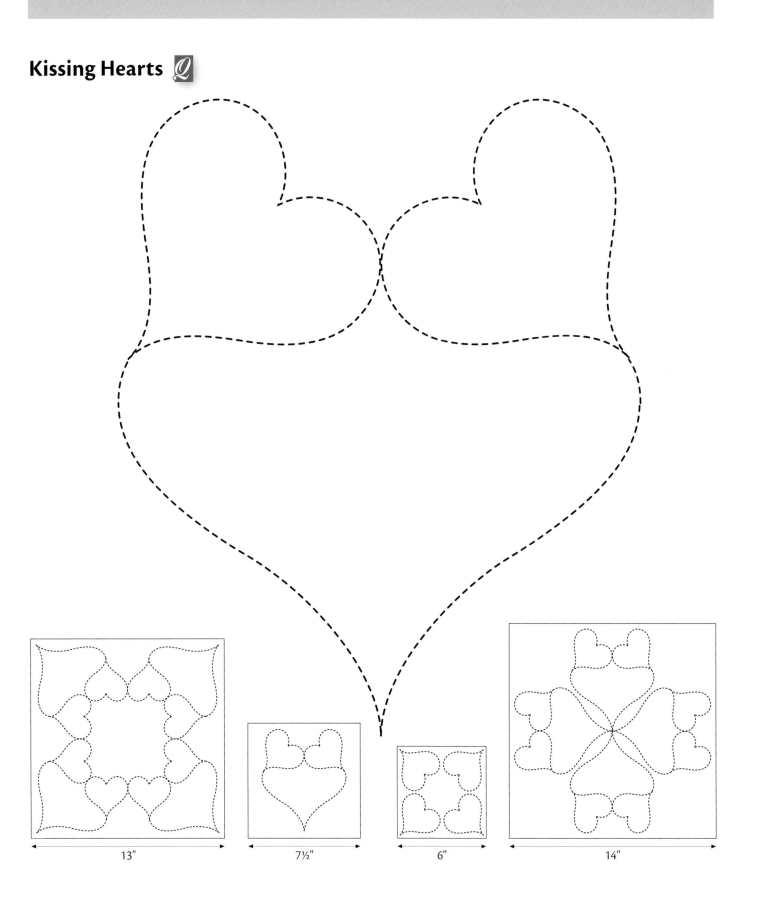

Hearts in Bloom 1

For single heart shape, trace the heart that forms the flower.

4½"

6"

6½"

8½"

4"

3½"

8"

Hearts in Bloom 2

6½"

10½"

9"

8½"

Flower and Beehive

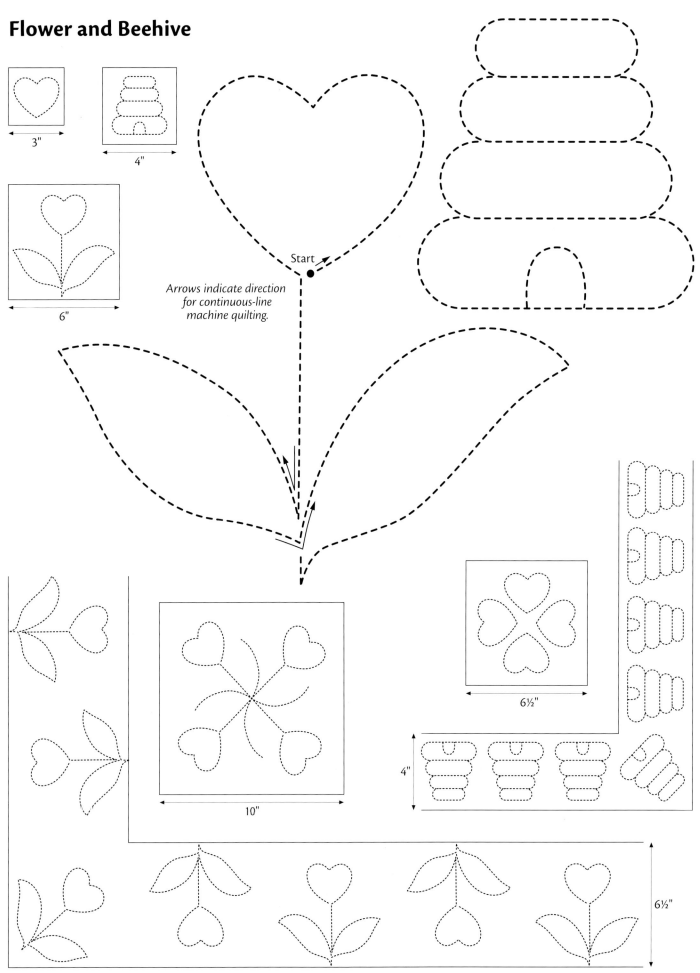

3"

4"

6"

Start

Arrows indicate direction
for continuous-line
machine quilting.

6½"

4"

10"

6½"

Love's Bloom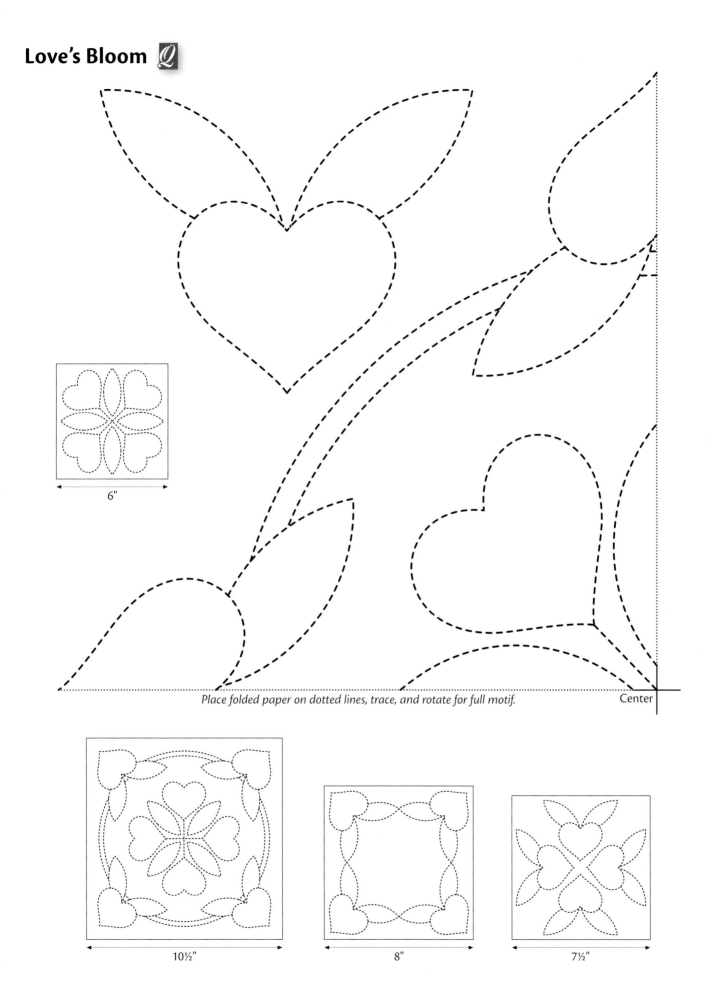

Place folded paper on dotted lines, trace, and rotate for full motif.

Center

6"

10½"

8"

7½"

April Love

Hearts and Flowers

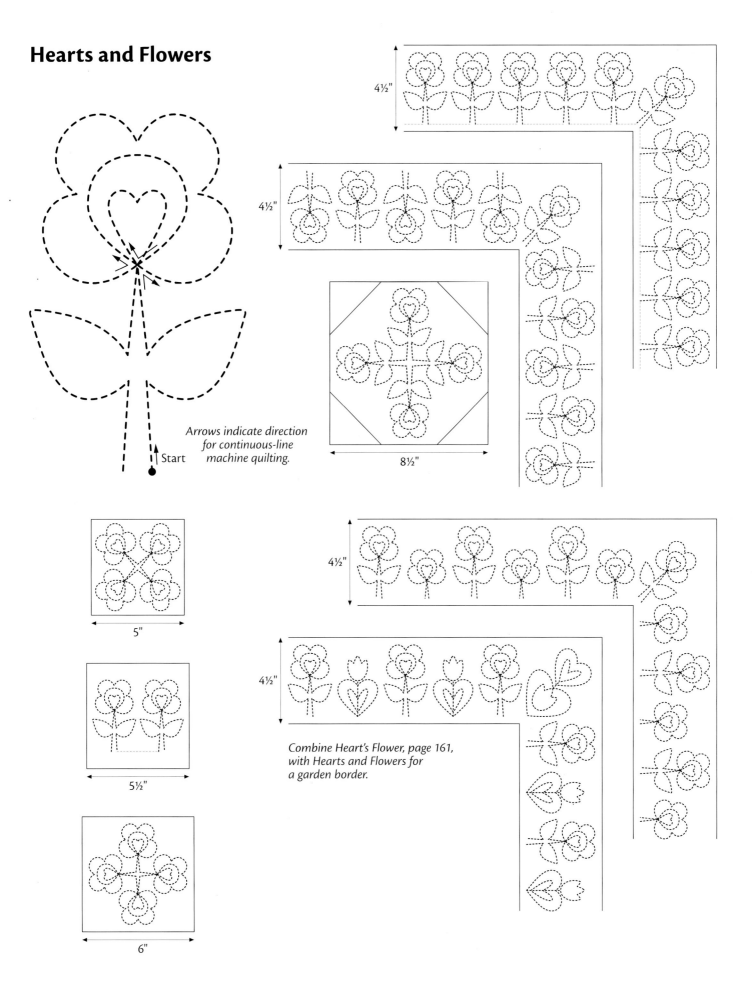

Arrows indicate direction for continuous-line machine quilting.

Start

4½"

4½"

8½"

5"

5½"

6"

4½"

4½"

Combine Heart's Flower, page 161, with Hearts and Flowers for a garden border.

Hearts and Swags

4"

4"

4"

Center

Place folded paper on dotted lines, trace, and rotate for full motif.

5½"

5½"

5½"

15"

11"

11"

10"

Floral Heart

Loving Hearts

Place folded paper on dotted line, trace, and rotate for full motif

7"

10½"

5½"

4½"

3½"

14"

Amish Traditions

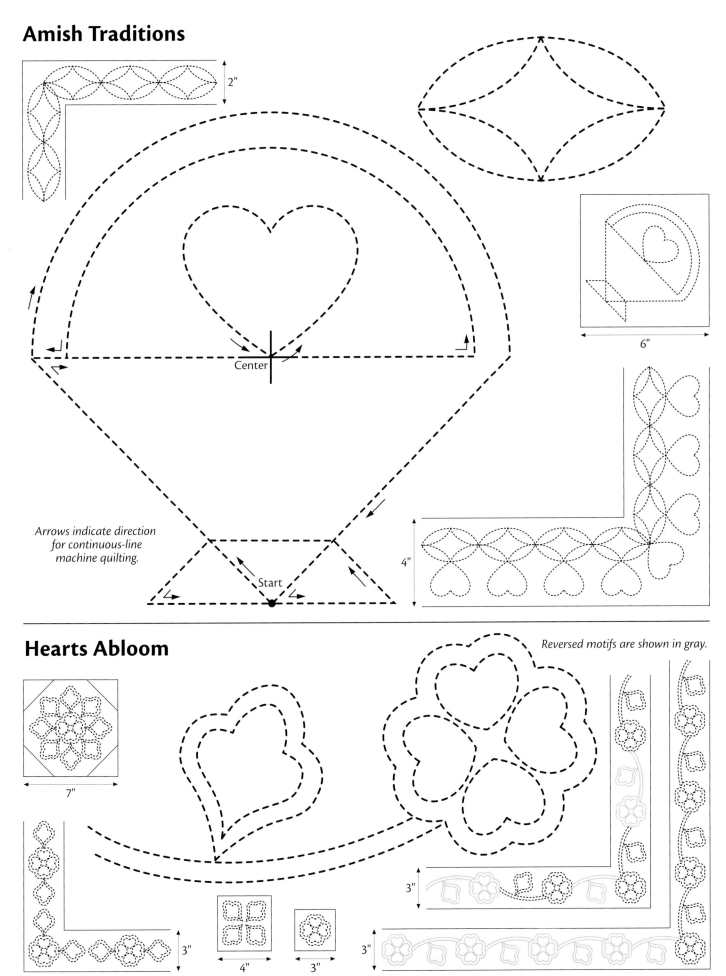

2"

Center

Start

Arrows indicate direction
for continuous-line
machine quilting.

6"

4"

Hearts Abloom

Reversed motifs are shown in gray.

7"

3"

3"

4"   3"

3"

Grace Notes

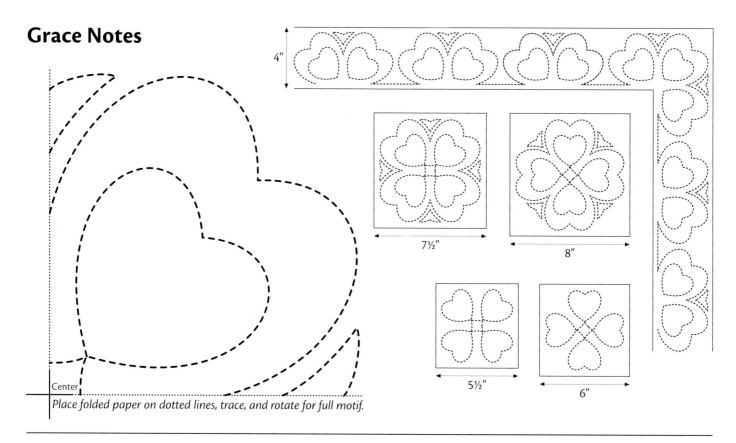

Center

Place folded paper on dotted lines, trace, and rotate for full motif.

4"

7½"

8"

5½"

6"

Heartsong

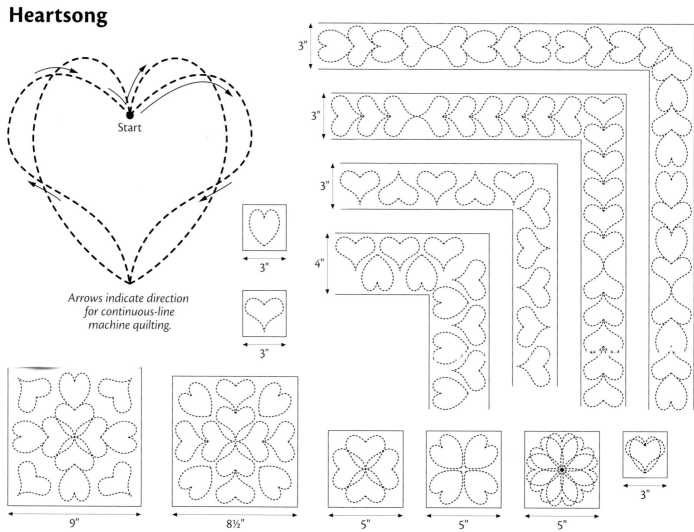

Start

Arrows indicate direction for continuous-line machine quilting.

3"

3"

3"

3"

3"

4"

9"

8½"

5"

5"

5"

3"

Ribbons of Love

4½"

4½"

16"

Place folded paper on dotted line, trace, and flip for full motif.

4½"

13"

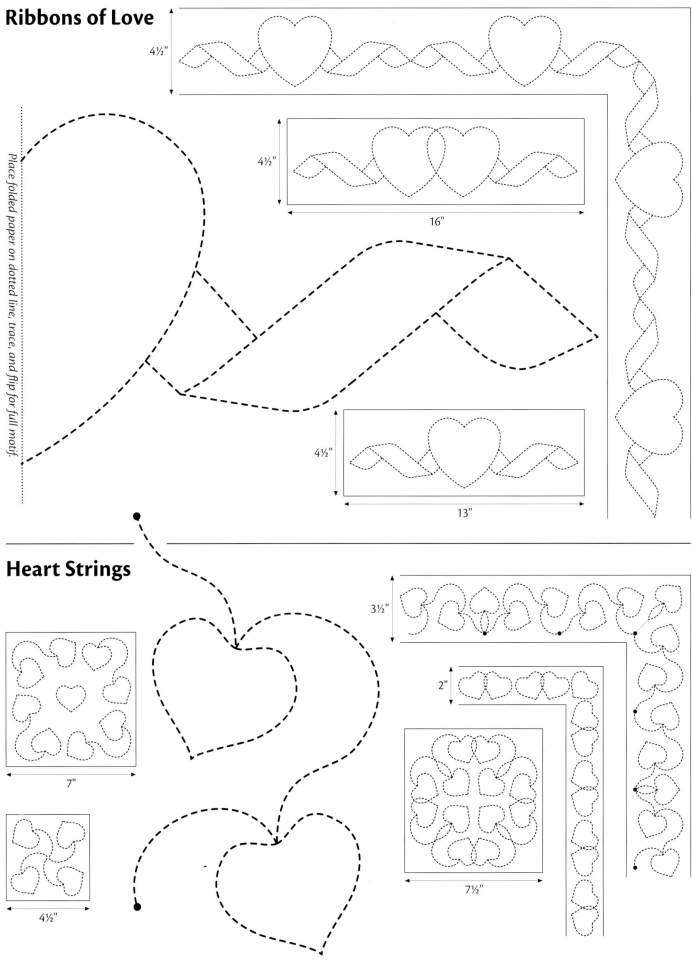

Heart Strings

7"

4½"

3½"

2"

7½"

Rhythm and Bows

Place folded paper on dotted line, trace, and flip for full motif.

7½"

4"

3½"

11½"

5½"

9"

8½"

8½"

Hearts Around

Place folded paper on dotted line, trace, and rotate for full motif.

9"

3½"

8½"

6"

Heart Songs

6½"

6½"

3½"

4½"

3½"

3"

5½"

9½"

Caesar's Heart 𝒬

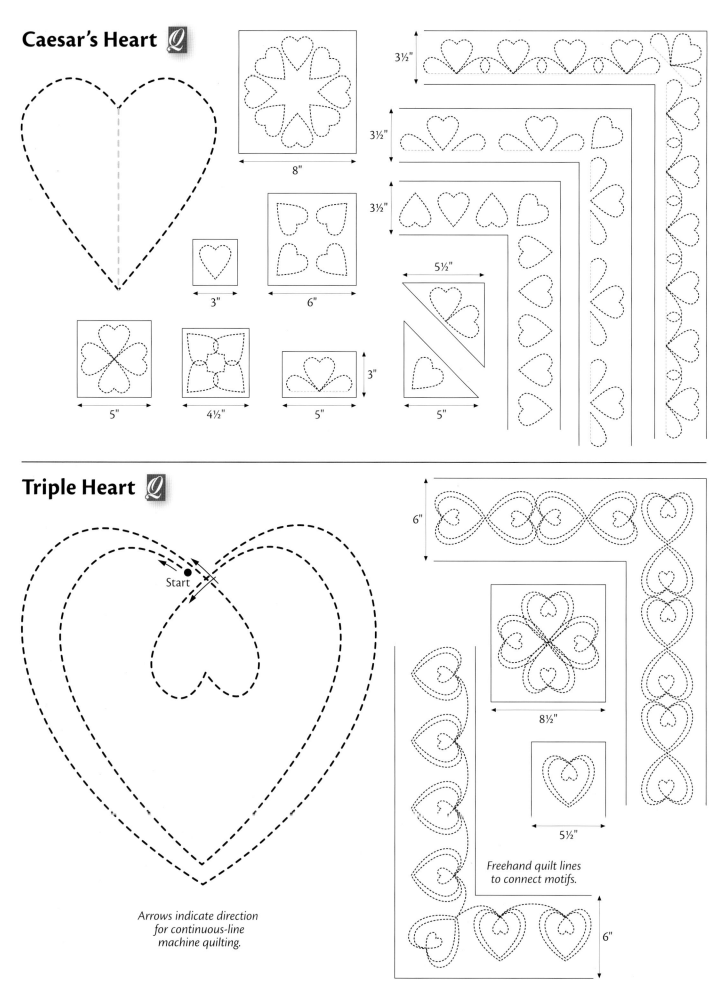

8"

3½"

3½"

3½"

3"

6"

5½"

5"

4½"

5"

3"

5"

Triple Heart 𝒬

Start

*Arrows indicate direction
for continuous-line
machine quilting.*

6"

8½"

5½"

6"

*Freehand quilt lines
to connect motifs.*

Hearts Aflutter

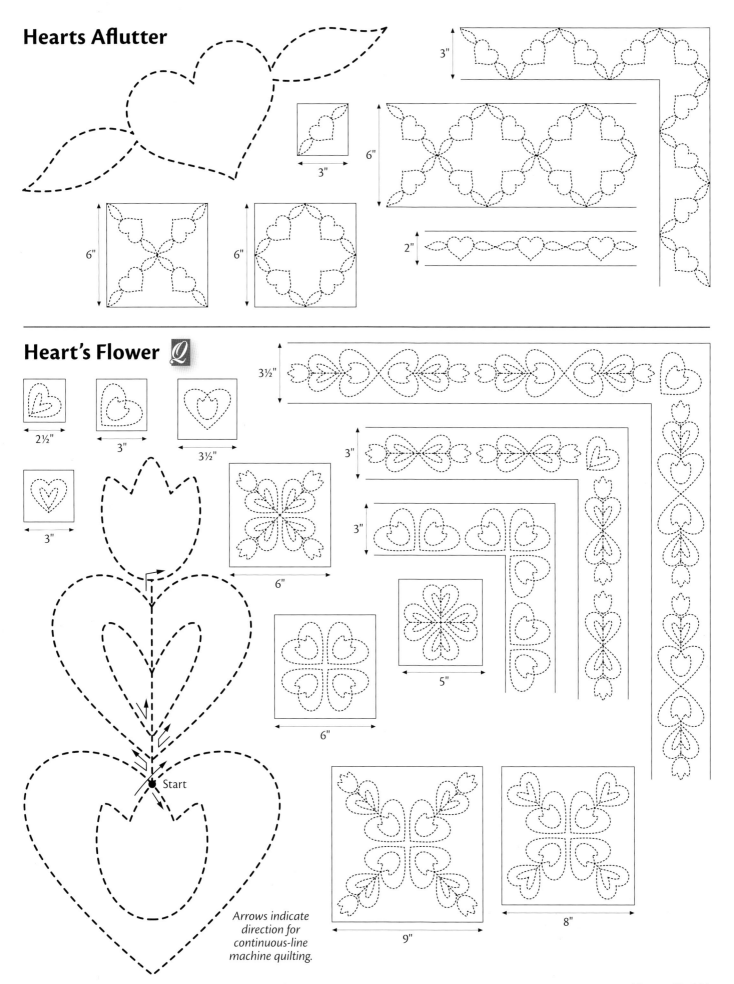

Heart's Flower

2½"

3"

3½"

3"

3½"

3"

3"

6"

6"

6"

2"

6"

6"

5"

6"

9"

8"

Arrows indicate direction for continuous-line machine quilting.

Start

Spring Delight

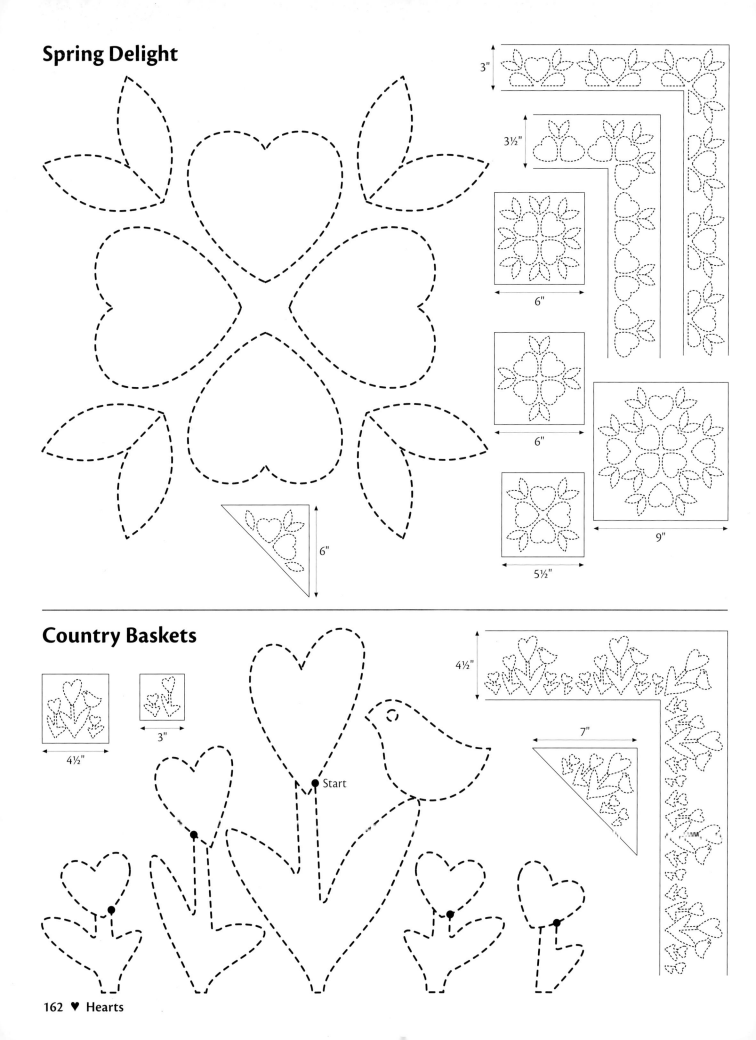

3"

3½"

6"

6"

9"

5½"

6"

Country Baskets

4½"

3"

4½"

Start

7"

Bows and Bells

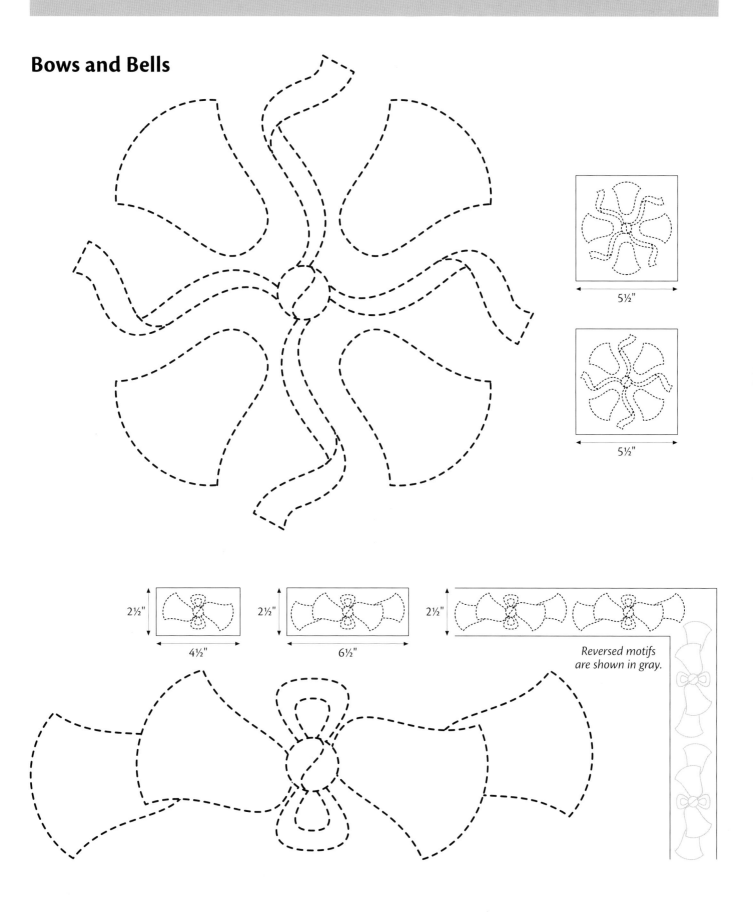

5½"

5½"

2½"

4½"

2½"

6½"

2½"

*Reversed motifs
are shown in gray.*

Simply Snowflakes

5"

3½"

5"

5"

10"

Holiday Hearts

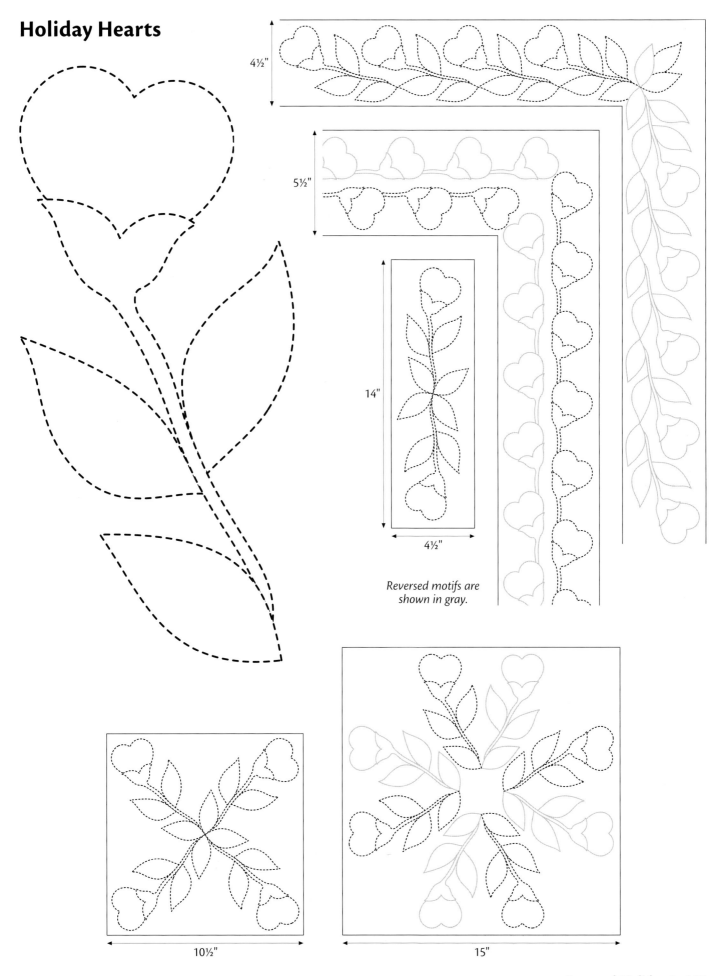

Reversed motifs are shown in gray.

4½"

5½"

14"

4½"

10½"

15"

Patch-o'-Pumpkins

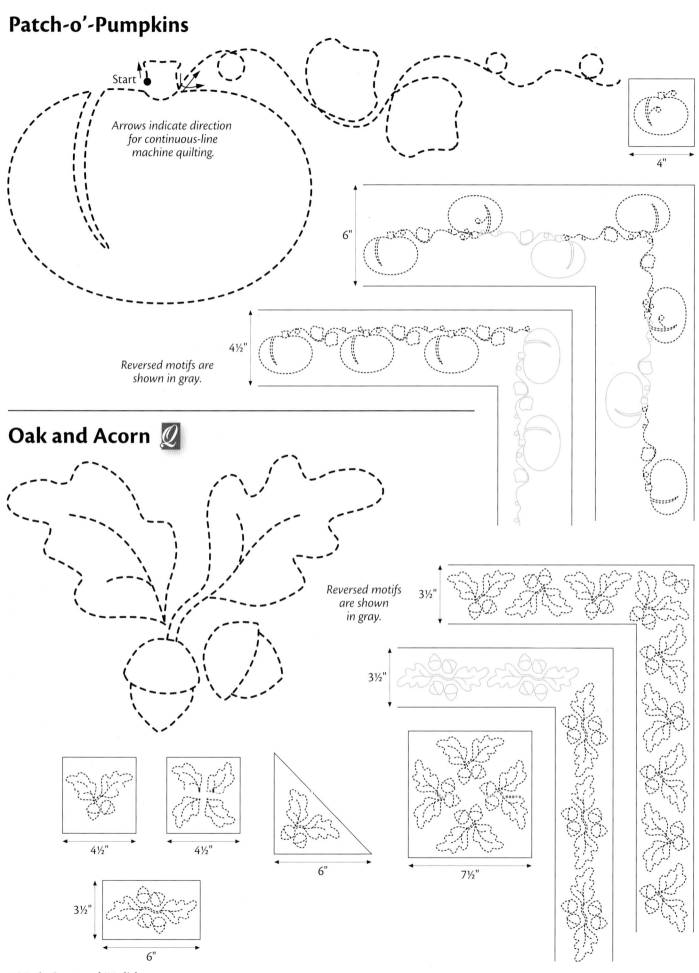

Start

Arrows indicate direction
for continuous-line
machine quilting.

4"

6"

4½"

*Reversed motifs are
shown in gray.*

Oak and Acorn

*Reversed motifs
are shown
in gray.*

3½"

3½"

4½"

4½"

6"

7½"

3½"

6"

Pumpkin Vine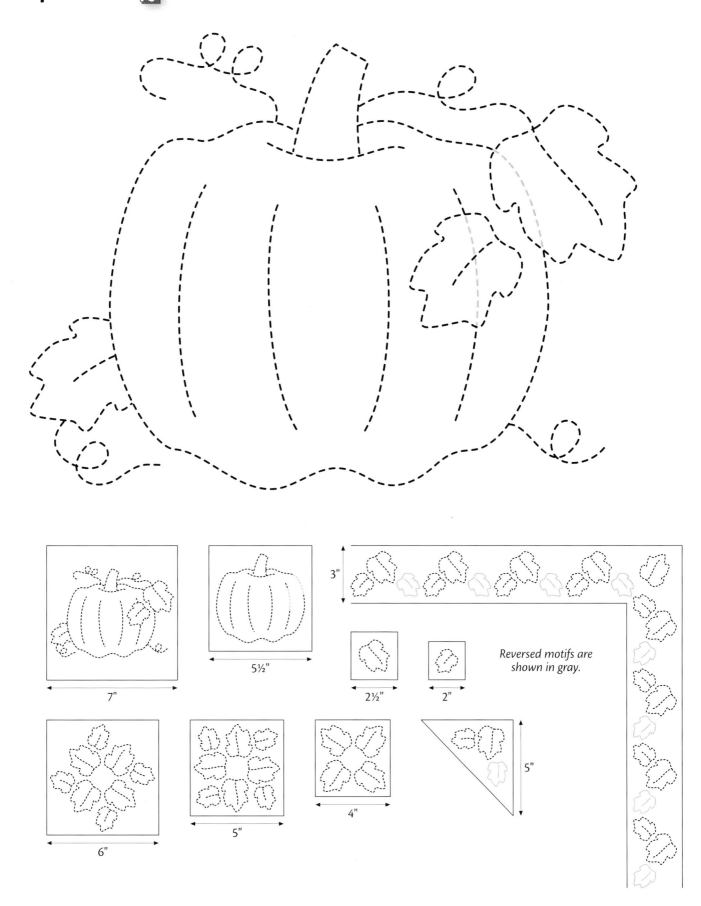

Reversed motifs are
shown in gray.

7"

5½"

3"

2½"

2"

6"

5"

4"

5"

Starburst Q

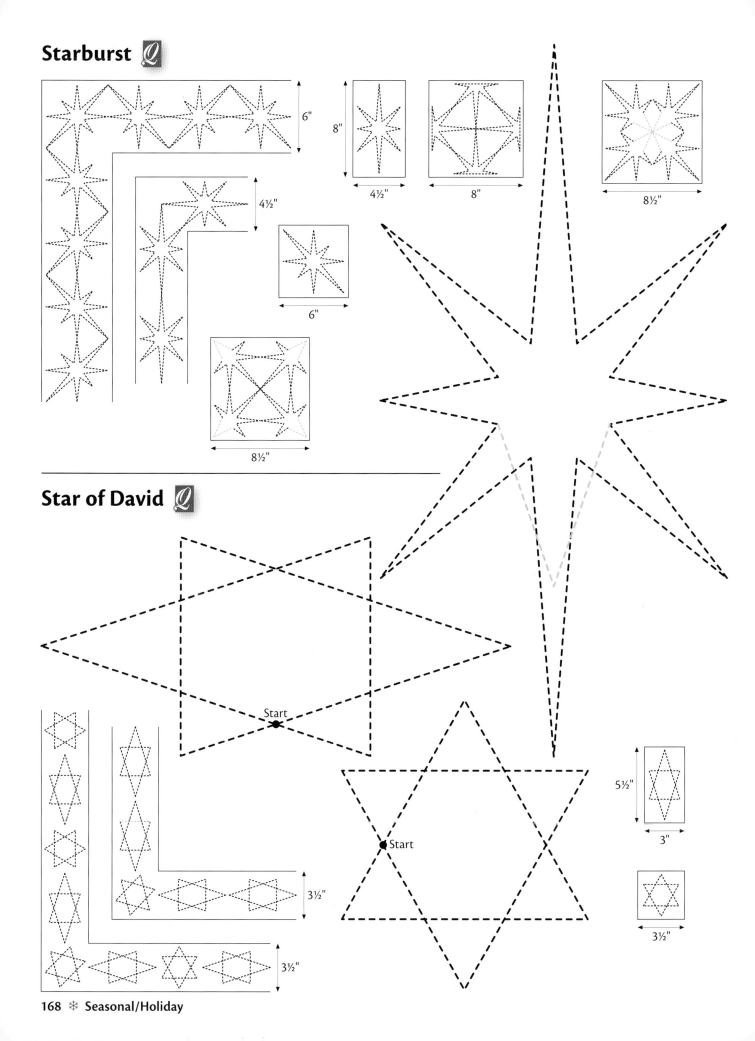

6"

8"

4½"

8"

8½"

4½"

6"

8½"

Star of David Q

Start

Start

5½"

3"

3½"

3½"

3½"

3½"

Piney Woods

Heavenly Dove

Arrow indicates direction for continuous-line machine quilting.

Start

Reversed motifs are shown in gray.

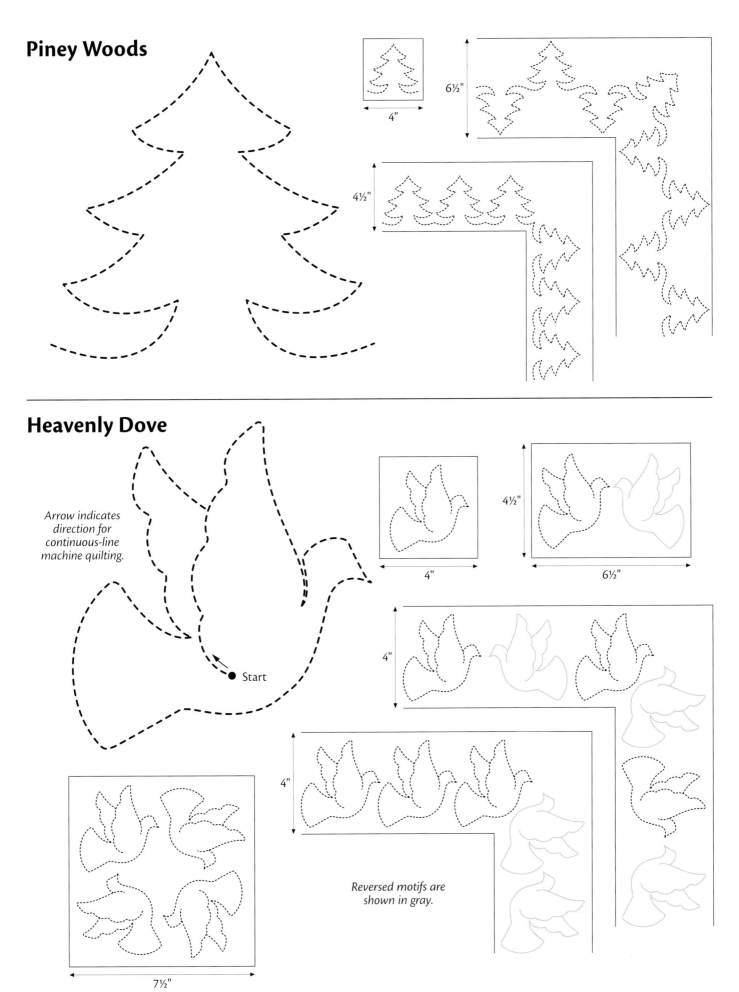

Poinsettia Garland

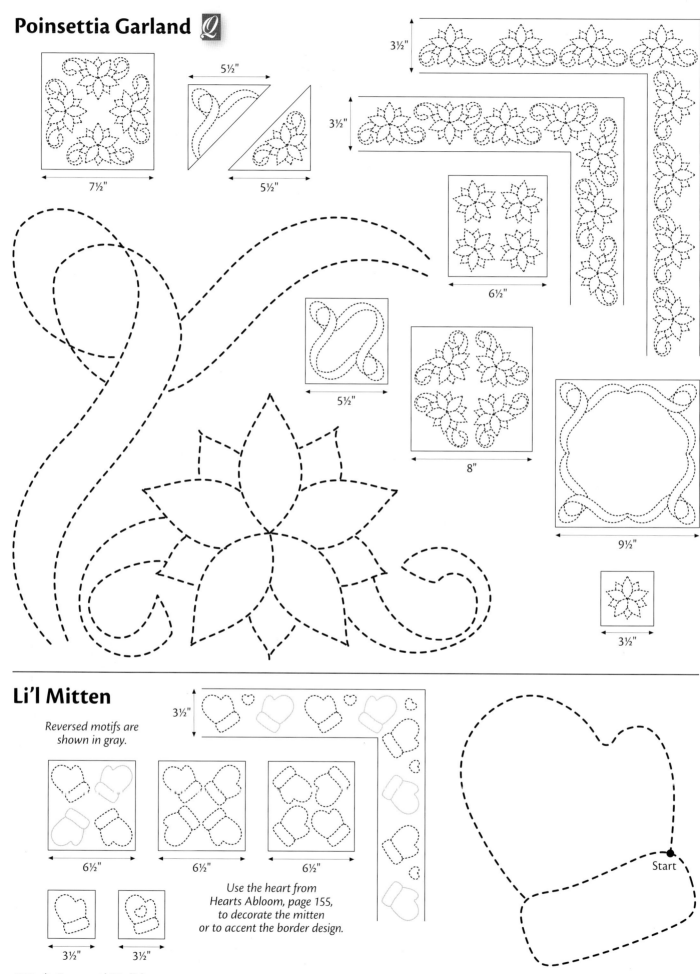

7½"

5½"

5½"

3½"

3½"

6½"

5½"

8"

9½"

3½"

Li'l Mitten

Reversed motifs are shown in gray.

3½"

6½"

6½"

6½"

Use the heart from *Hearts Abloom*, page 155, to decorate the mitten or to accent the border design.

3½"

3½"

Start

Poinsettia Wreath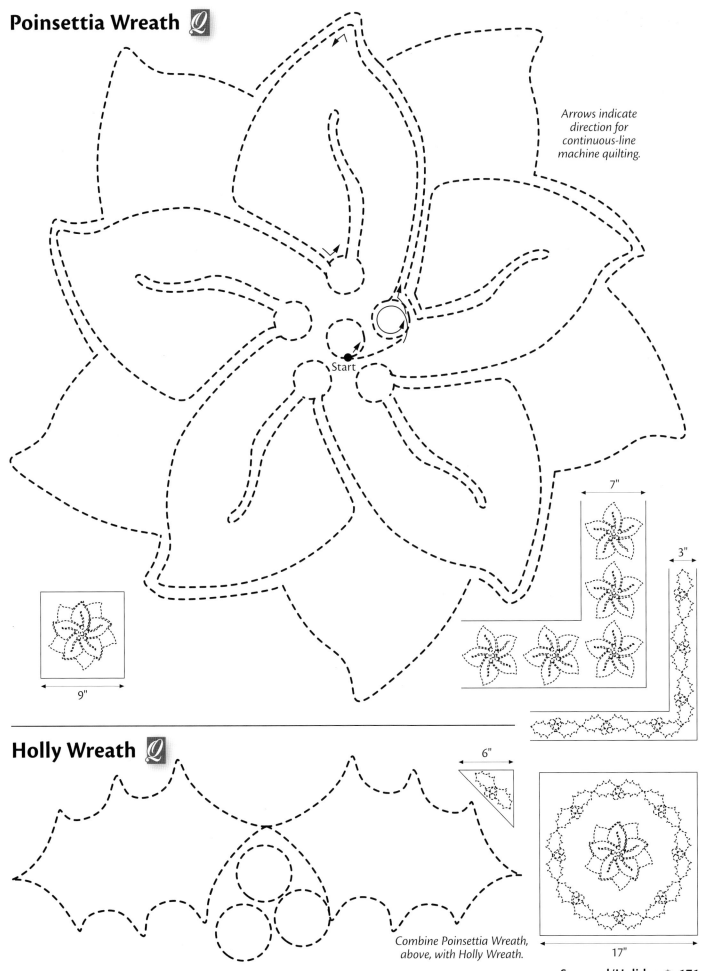

Arrows indicate direction for continuous-line machine quilting.

Start

7"

3"

9"

Holly Wreath

6"

Combine Poinsettia Wreath, above, with Holly Wreath.

17"

Holly and Ribbon Q

Start

Arrows indicate direction for continuous-line machine quilting.

8"

8"

8"

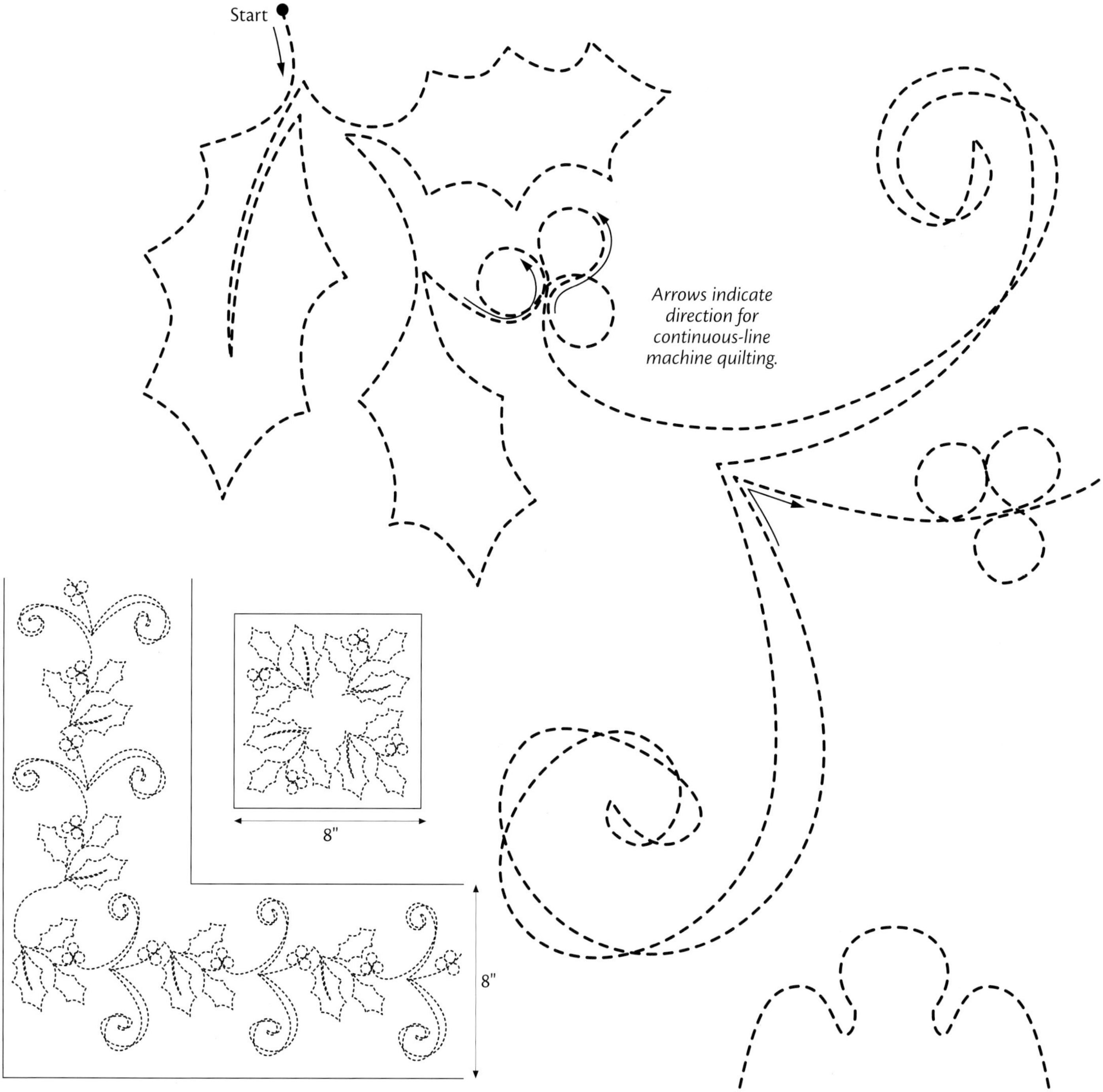

Angel

4"

7"

7"

3½"

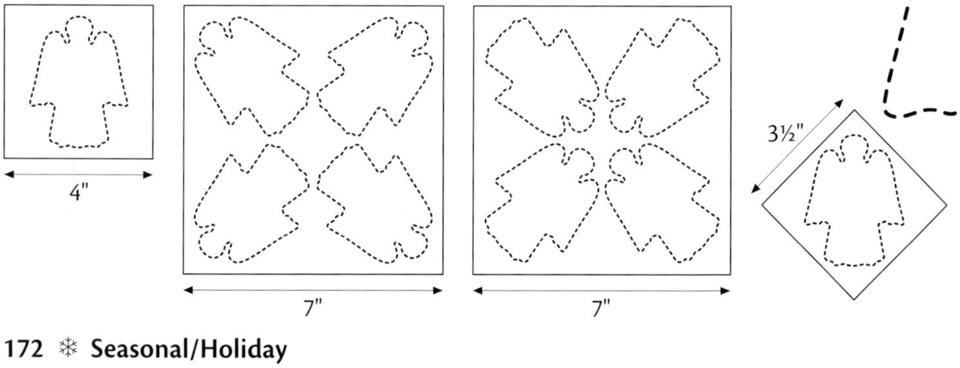

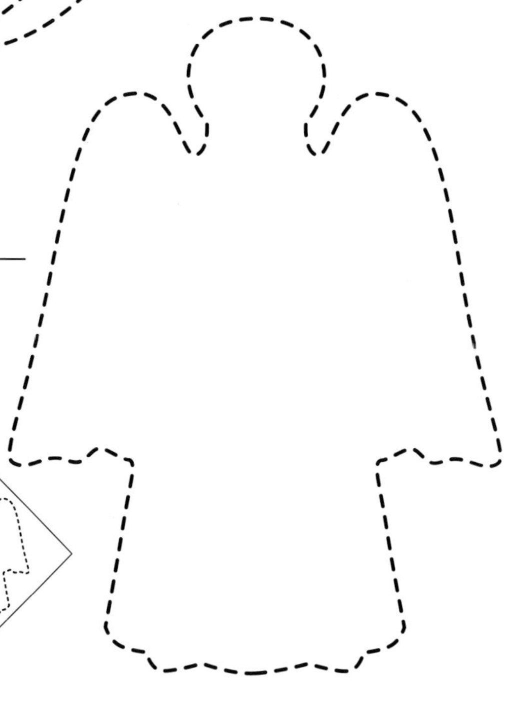

Poinsettia

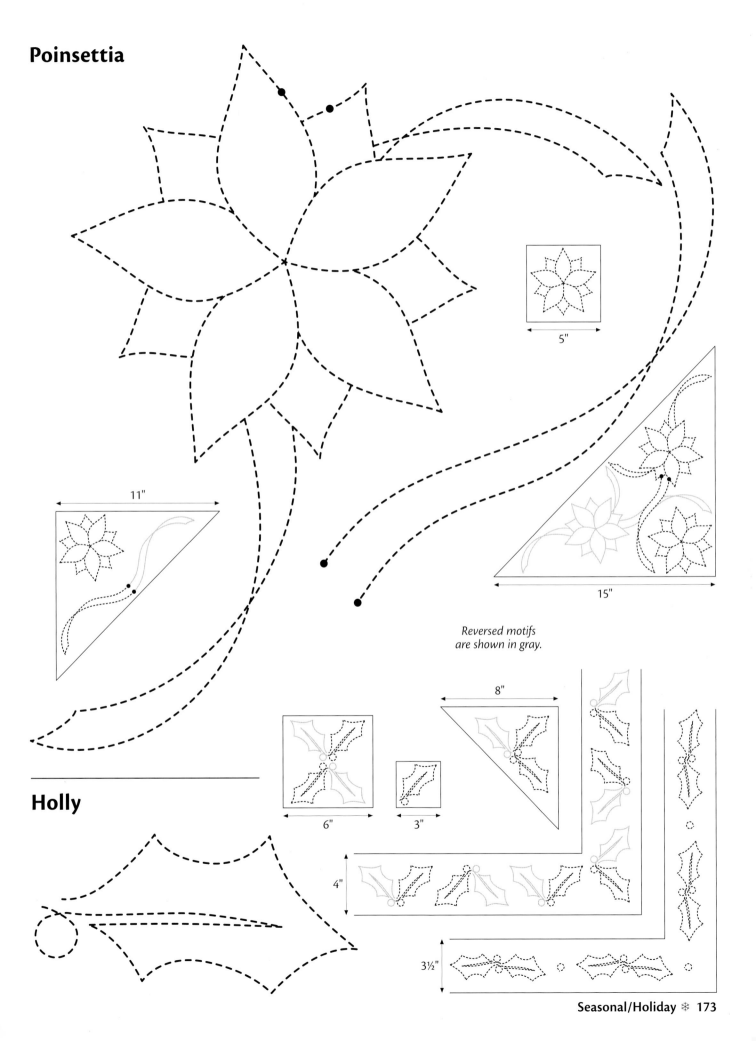

5"

11"

15"

Reversed motifs are shown in gray.

Holly

8"

6"

3"

4"

3½"

Hollyberry

Christmas Lights

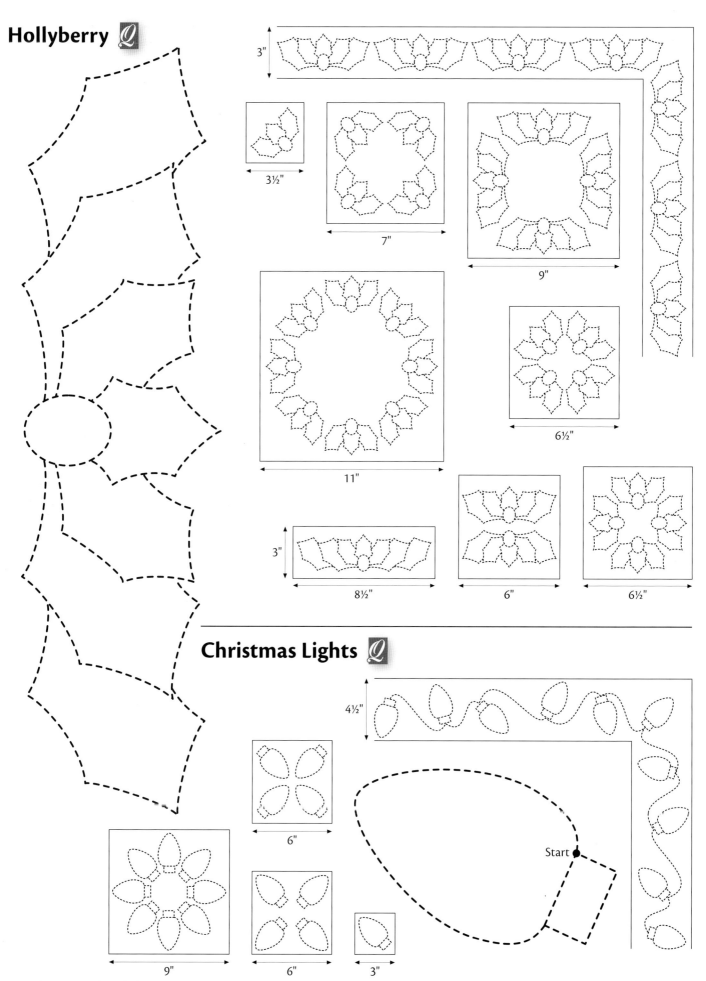

Bow Tie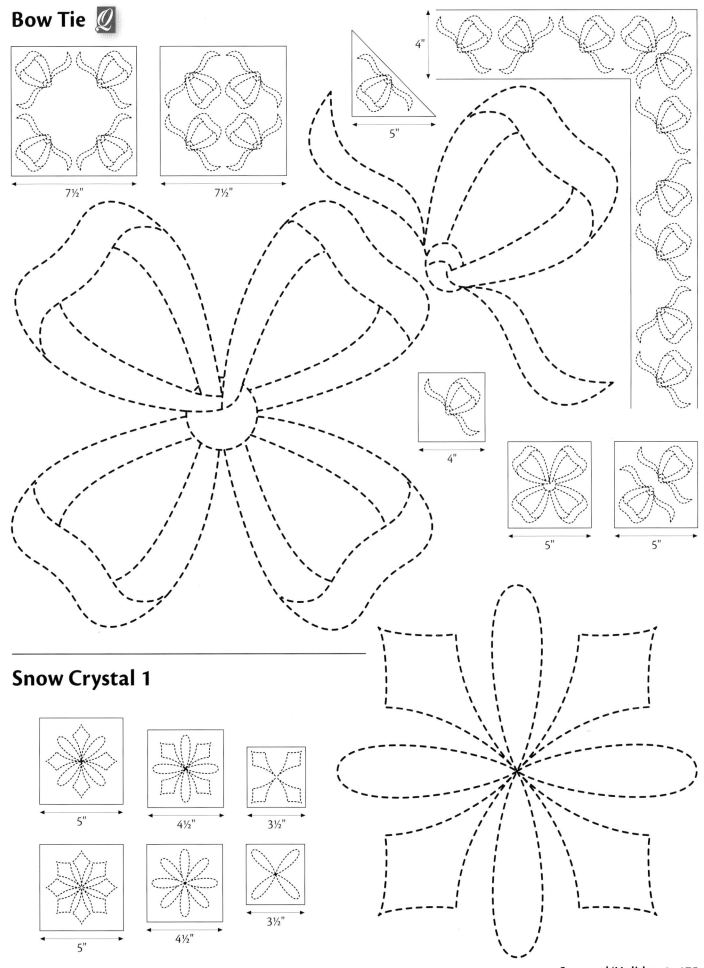

7½"

7½"

4"

5"

4"

5"   5"

Snow Crystal 1

5"   4½"   3½"

5"   4½"   3½"

Snow Crystal 2

Snowflake

Vines and Leaves

Grapevine

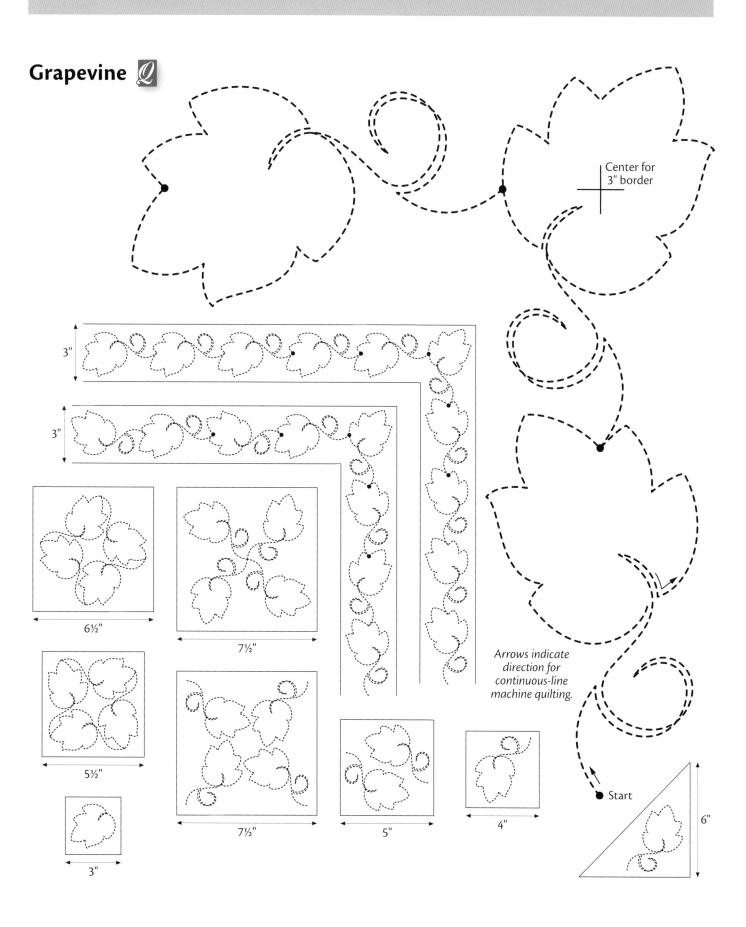

Center for 3" border

3"

3"

6½"

7½"

5½"

7½"

3"

7½"

5"

4"

Arrows indicate direction for continuous-line machine quilting.

Start

6"

Leafy Vine

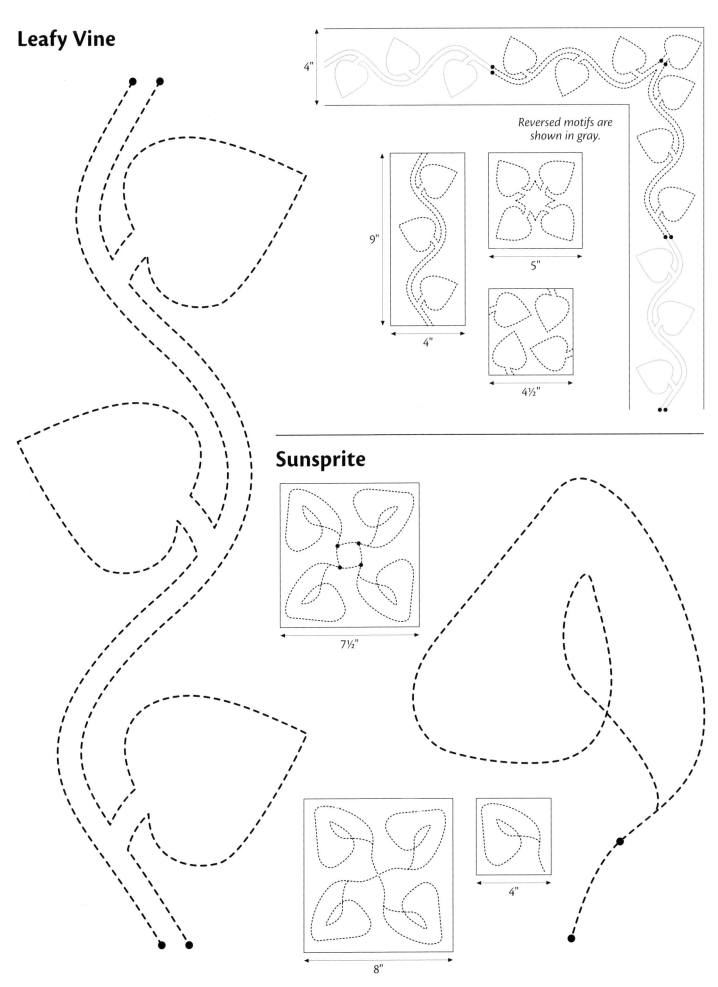

Reversed motifs are shown in gray.

4"

9"

4"

5"

4½"

Sunprite

7½"

8"

4"

Budding Vine

6"

3½"

12"

4"

6"

5"

4"

3½"

5½"

7½"

9"

10"

7"

8" (5" circle)

10"

5"

*Reversed motifs are
shown in gray.*

Ivy 1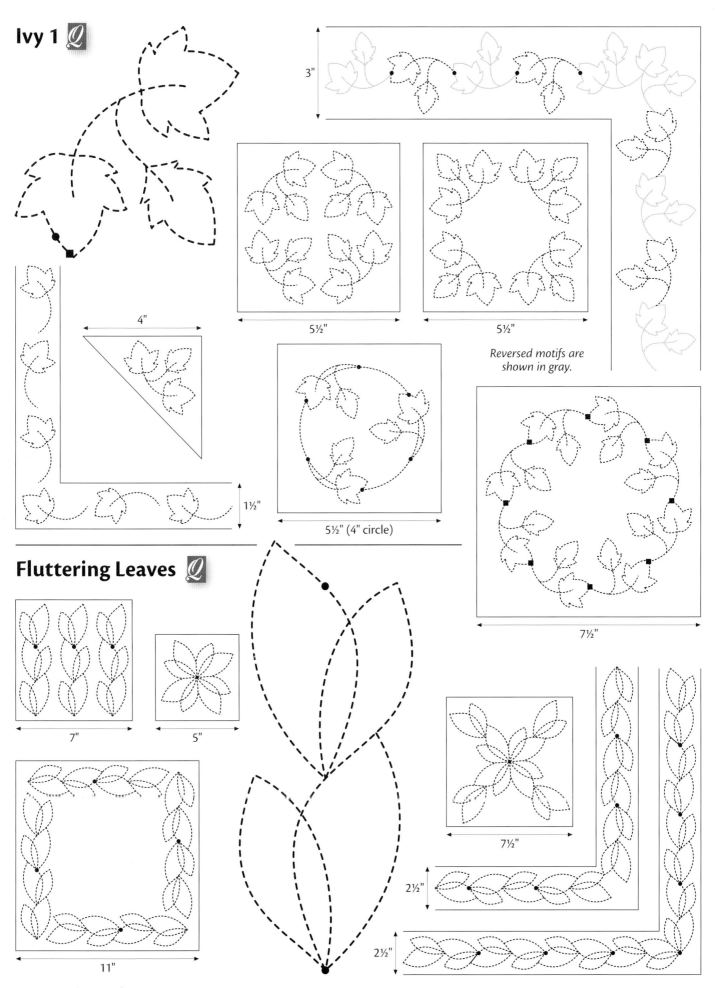

3"

5½"

5½"

4"

1½"

5½" (4" circle)

Reversed motifs are shown in gray.

7½"

Fluttering Leaves

7"

5"

7½"

11"

2½"

2½"

Versatile Ivy

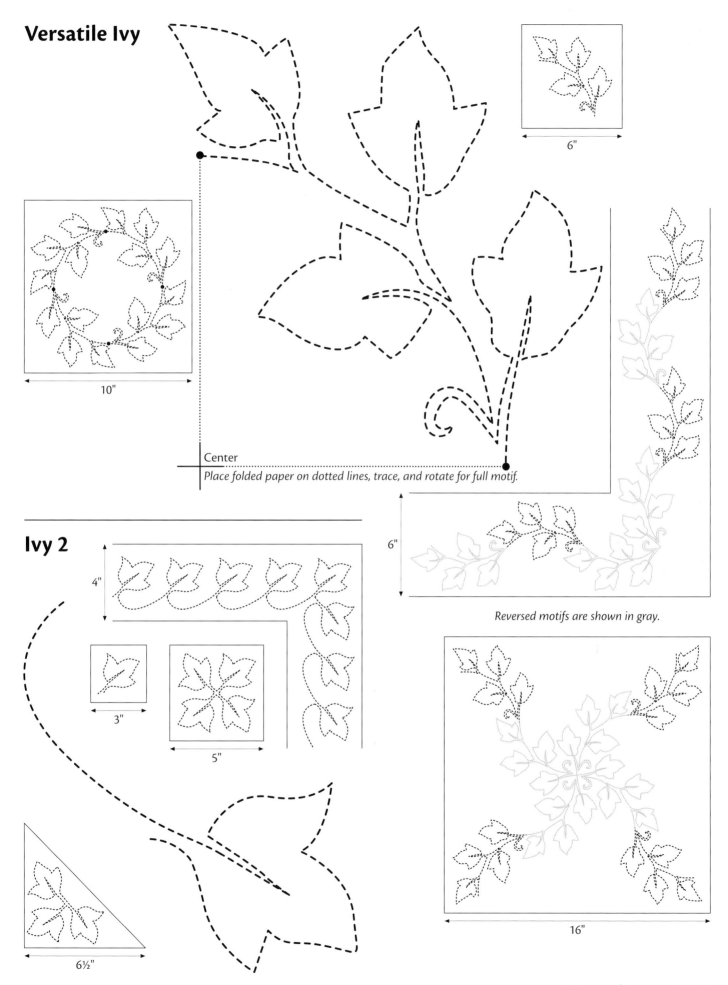

10"

6"

Center
Place folded paper on dotted lines, trace, and rotate for full motif.

6"

Reversed motifs are shown in gray.

Ivy 2

4"

3"

5"

6½"

16"

Leaf Cable

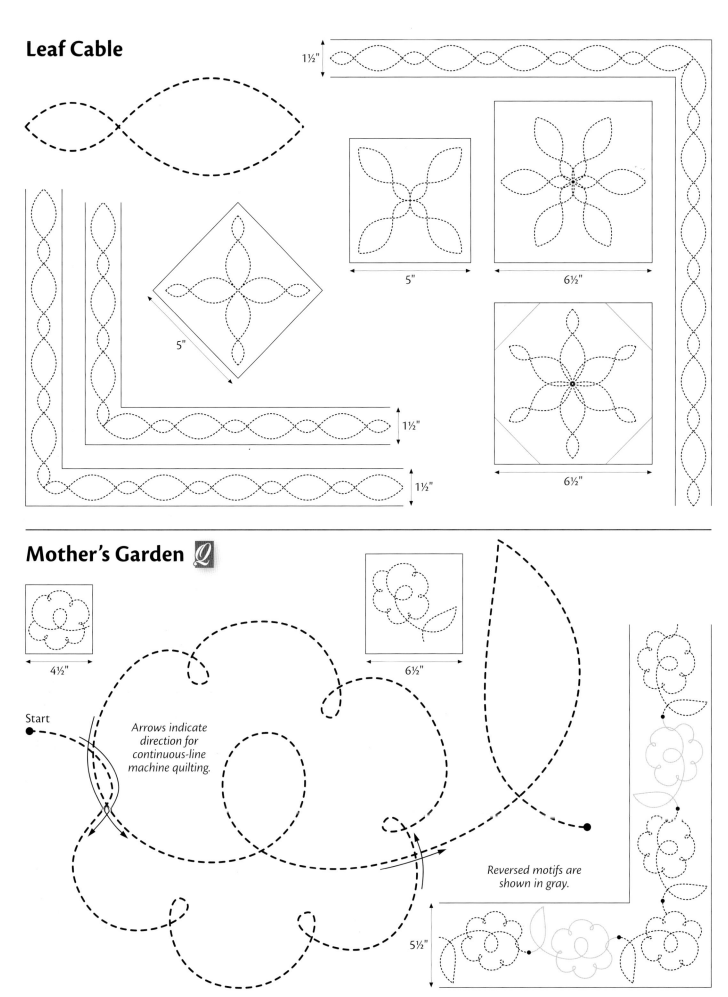

Mother's Garden

Arrows indicate direction for continuous-line machine quilting.

Start

Reversed motifs are shown in gray.

Autumn Leaves

Arrows indicate direction for continuous-line machine quilting.

Start

Reversed motifs are shown in gray.

4"

5½"

7"

4"

3½"

Bamboo

4"

9"

6½"

9"

Leaf Spray

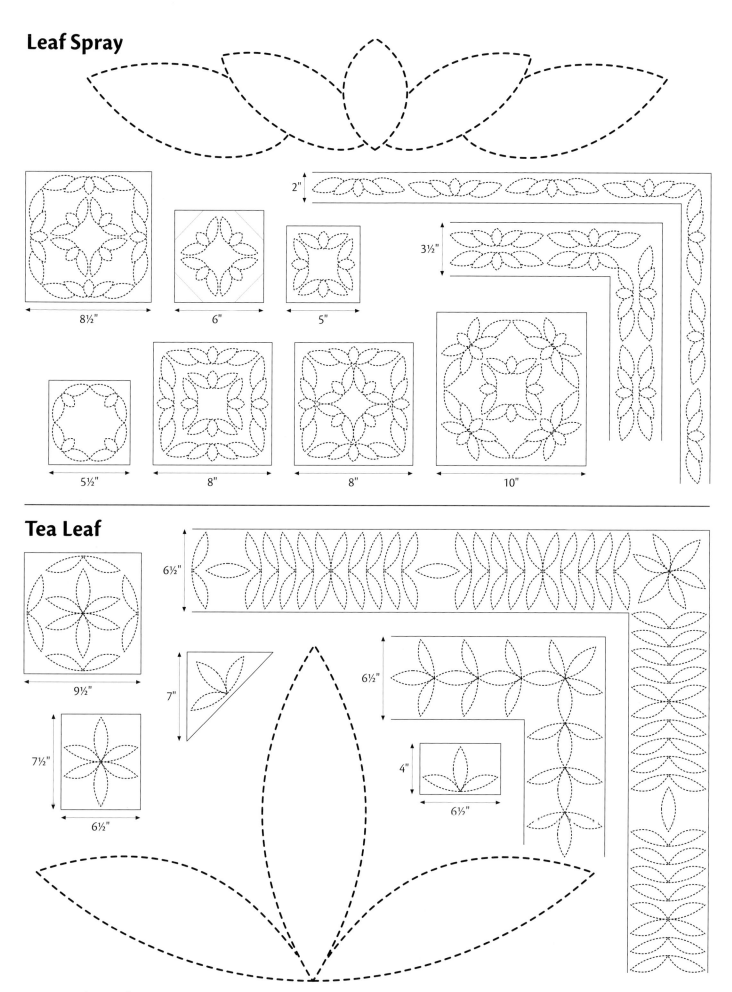

8½"

6"

5"

2"

3½"

5½"

8"

8"

10"

Tea Leaf

9½"

6½"

7"

6½"

7½"

6½"

4"

6½"

Woodland Sprig

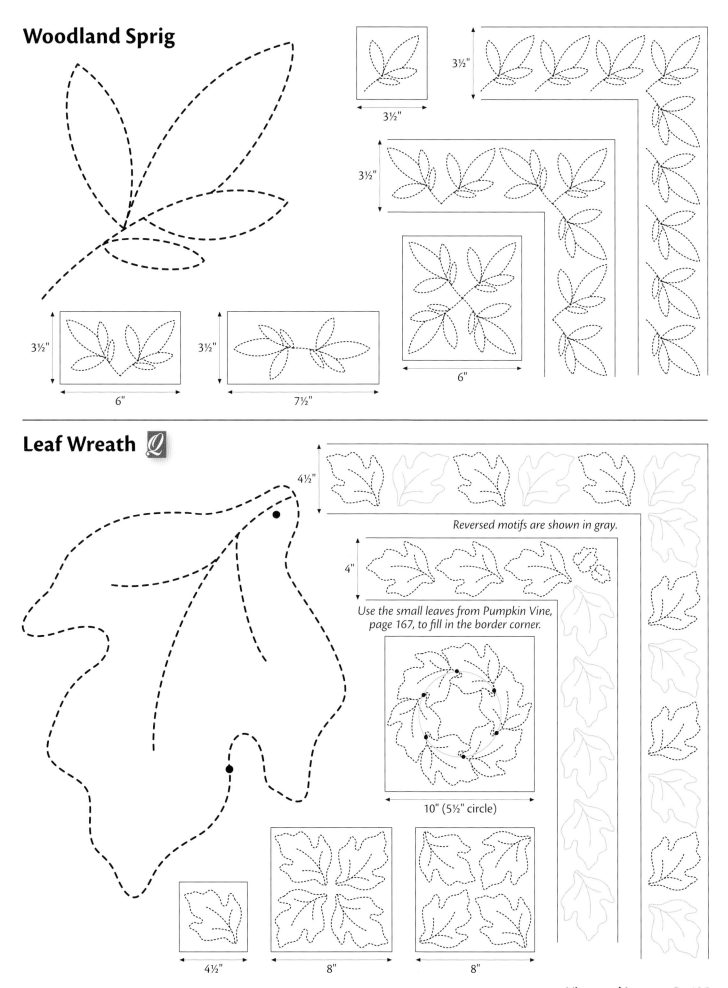

3½"

3½"

3½"

3½"

3½"

3½"

6"

6"

7½"

6"

Leaf Wreath

4½"

Reversed motifs are shown in gray.

4"

Use the small leaves from Pumpkin Vine, page 167, to fill in the border corner.

10" (5½" circle)

4½"

8"

8"

Lilting Leaf

Ivy League

Reversed motifs are shown in gray.

Fall Leaf

11" (6½" circle)

4"

4"

4"

4"

4"

7½"

7½"

7"

4"

4"

4"

13"

Trailing Vine

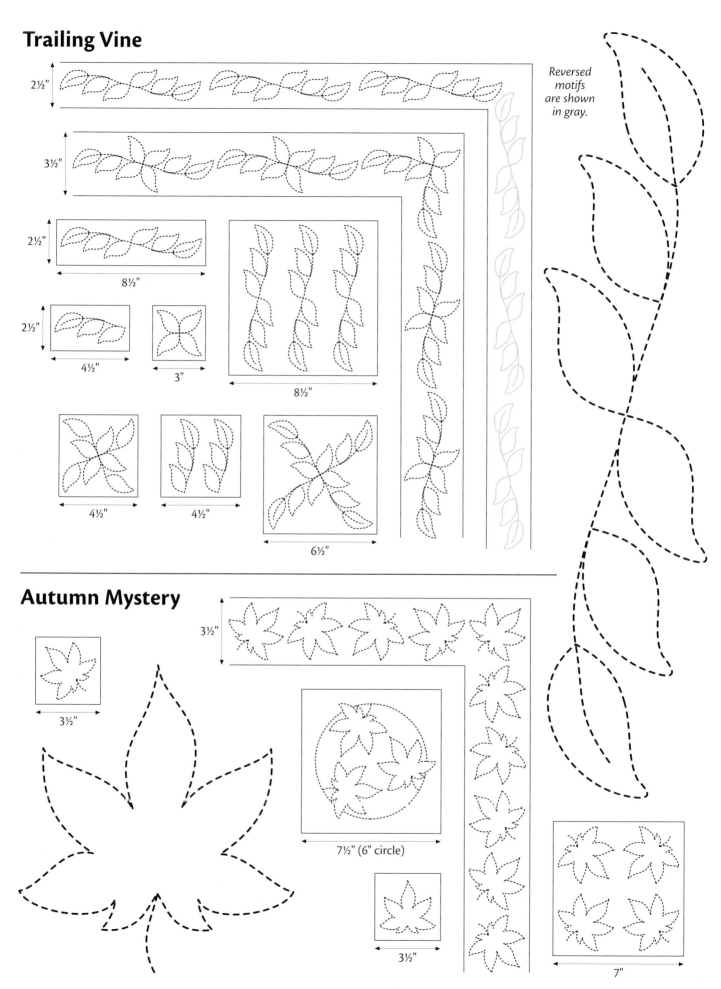

2½"

3½"

2½"

8½"

2½"

4½"

3"

8½"

2½"

4½"

4½"

6½"

Reversed motifs are shown in gray.

Autumn Mystery

3½"

3½"

7½" (6" circle)

3½"

7"

Fizz Leaves

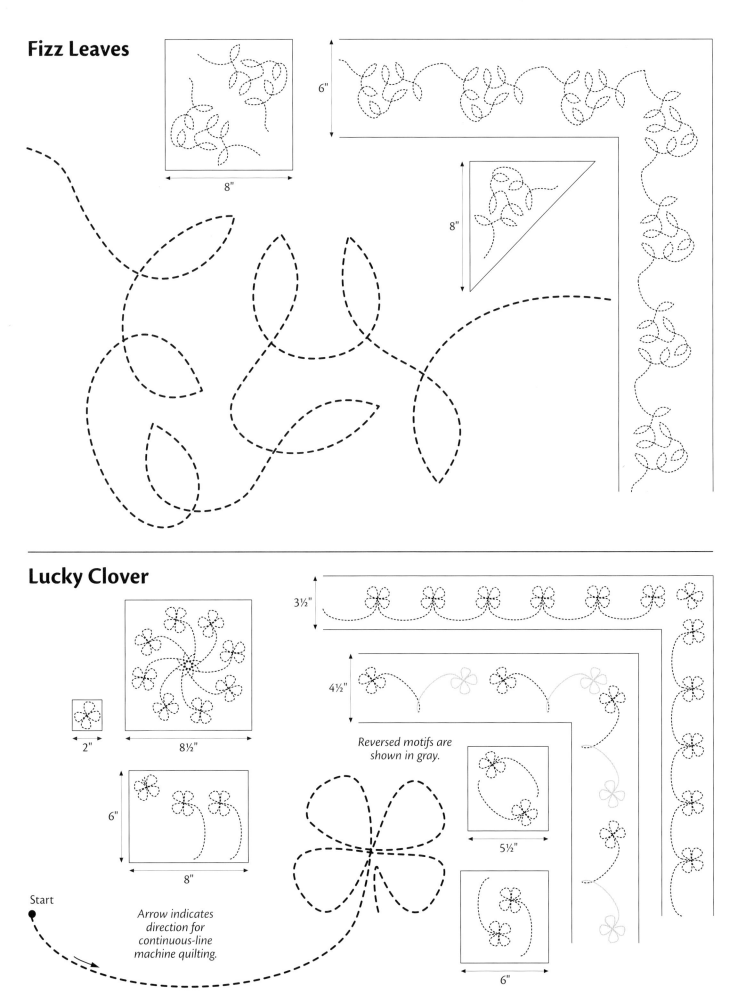

6"

8"

8"

Lucky Clover

3½"

4½"

Reversed motifs are shown in gray.

5½"

2"

8½"

6"

8"

6"

Start

Arrow indicates direction for continuous-line machine quilting.

Friendship Vine 1 Q

Freehand quilt lines to connect the leaves.

5"

8½"

8½"

11"

8½"

Reversed motifs are shown in gray.

Summer Leaves Q

2"

2"

9"

Combine Breezy Blossom, page 61, with Summer Leaves

Reversed motifs are shown in gray.

5"

6½"

9"

Friendship Vine 2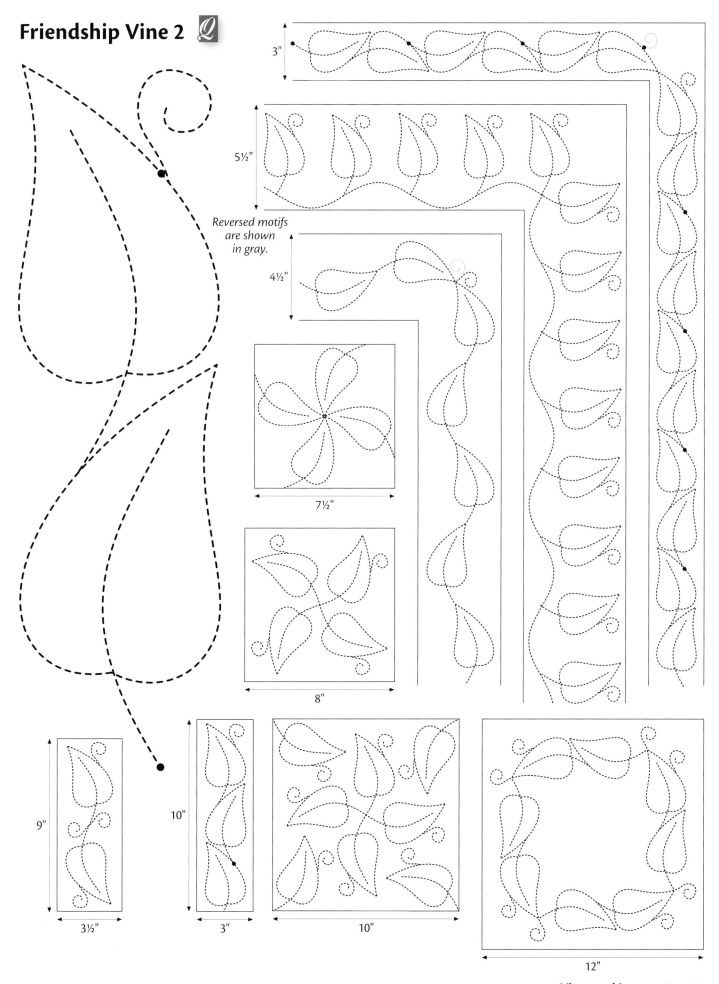

3"

5½"

*Reversed motifs
are shown
in gray.*

4½"

7½"

8"

9"

3½"

10"

3"

10"

12"

Spring Leaves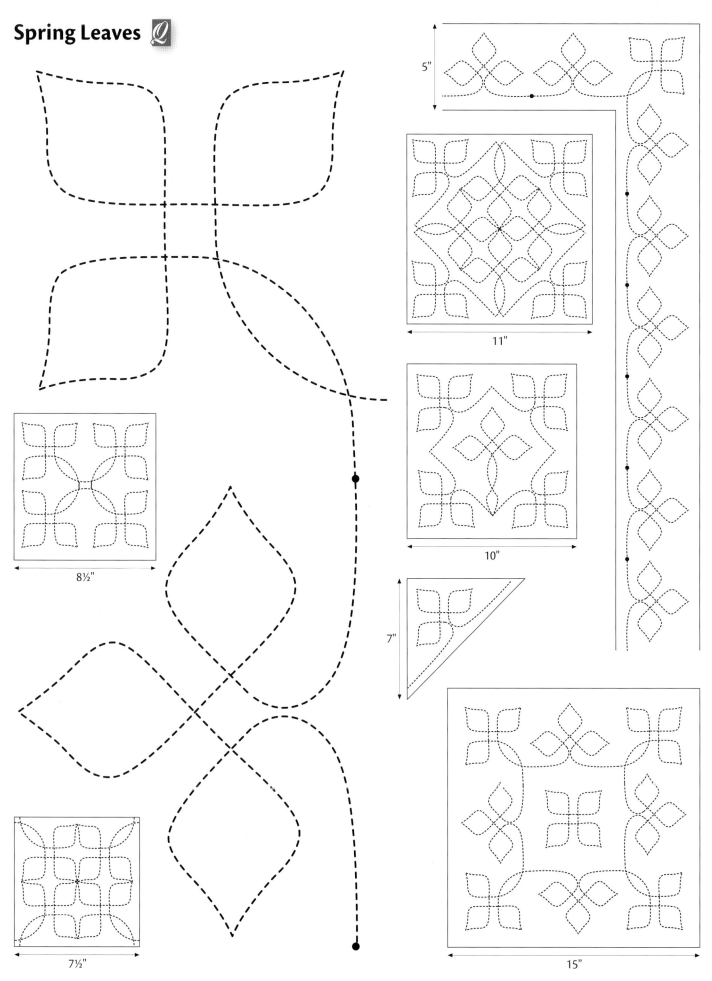

Loveleaf

Ivy Leaf

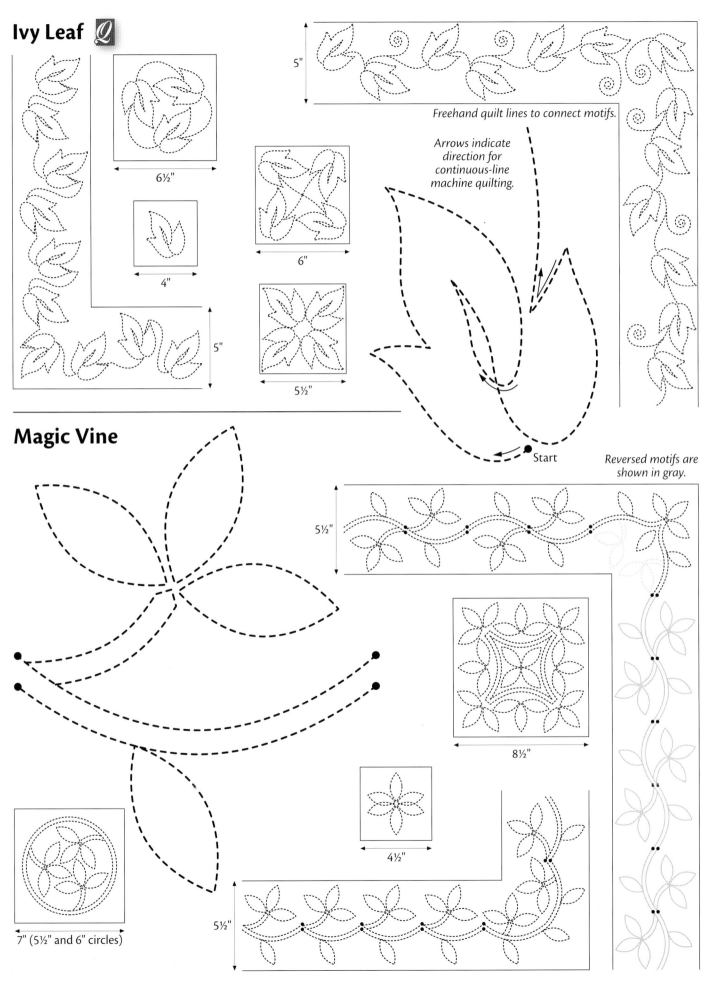

Freehand quilt lines to connect motifs.

Arrows indicate direction for continuous-line machine quilting.

6½"

4"

6"

5½"

5"

Start

Reversed motifs are shown in gray.

Magic Vine

5½"

8½"

4½"

5½"

7" (5½" and 6" circles)

Cloverleaf

4½"

4½"

3½"

2"

3½"

4"

4½"

3½"

4½"

3½"

4"

4½"

2½"

2½"

3"

Trellis Vine

Reversed motifs are shown in gray.

3"

8"

5"

6"

10½"

3"

12"

8"

10½"

10½"

Leafy Meander 1

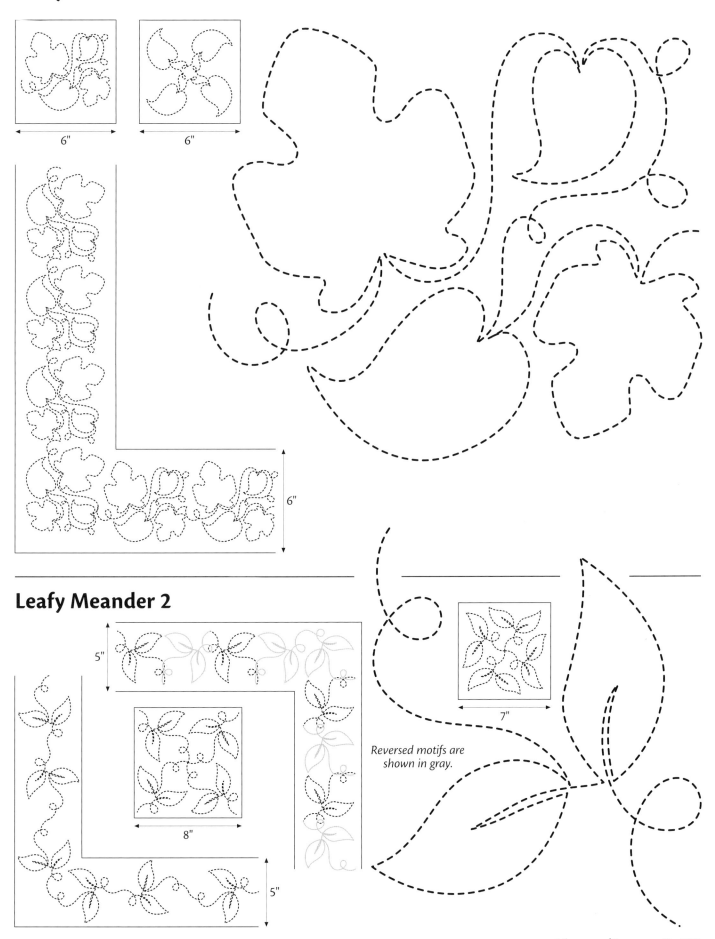

6"

6"

6"

Leafy Meander 2

5"

8"

5"

7"

*Reversed motifs are
shown in gray.*

Funky Flower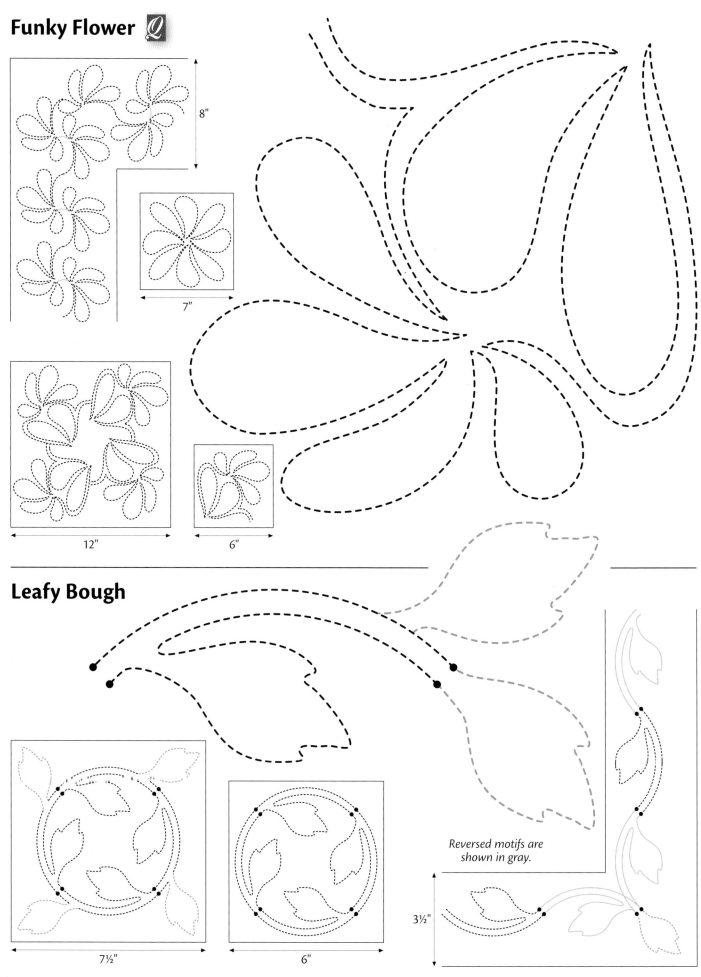

8"

7"

12"

6"

Leafy Bough

Reversed motifs are shown in gray.

3½"

7½"

6"

Lazy Leafy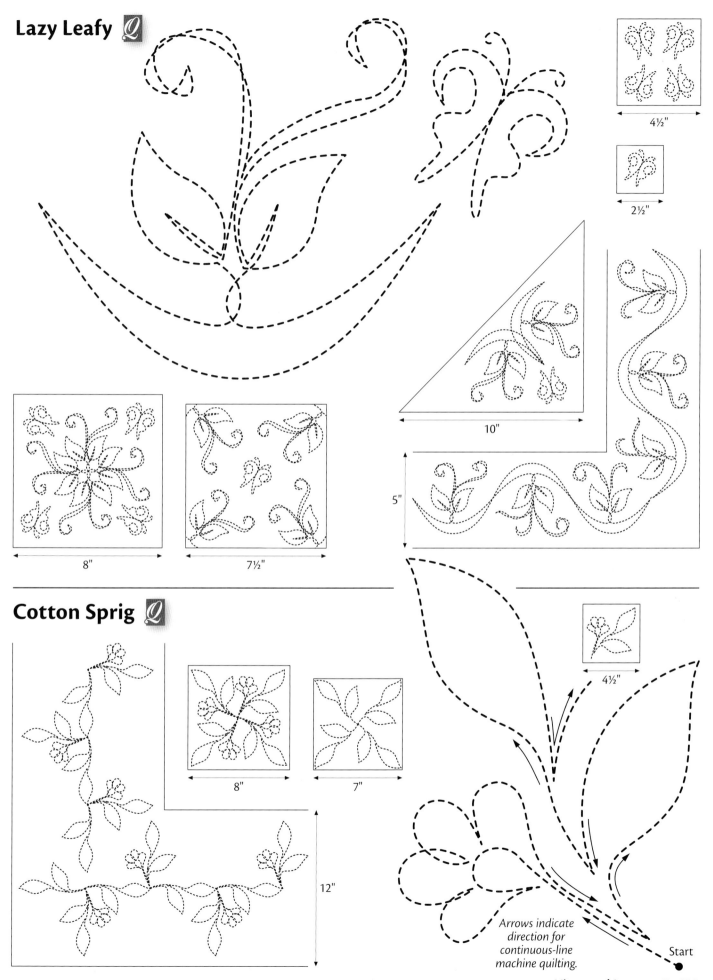

Cotton Sprig

Arrows indicate direction for continuous-line machine quilting.

Start

Lilac Leaf

3"

2½"

9"

6"

13"

6½"

10½"

8½"

9"

8"

Reversed motifs are shown in gray.

Circle and Angle Patterns

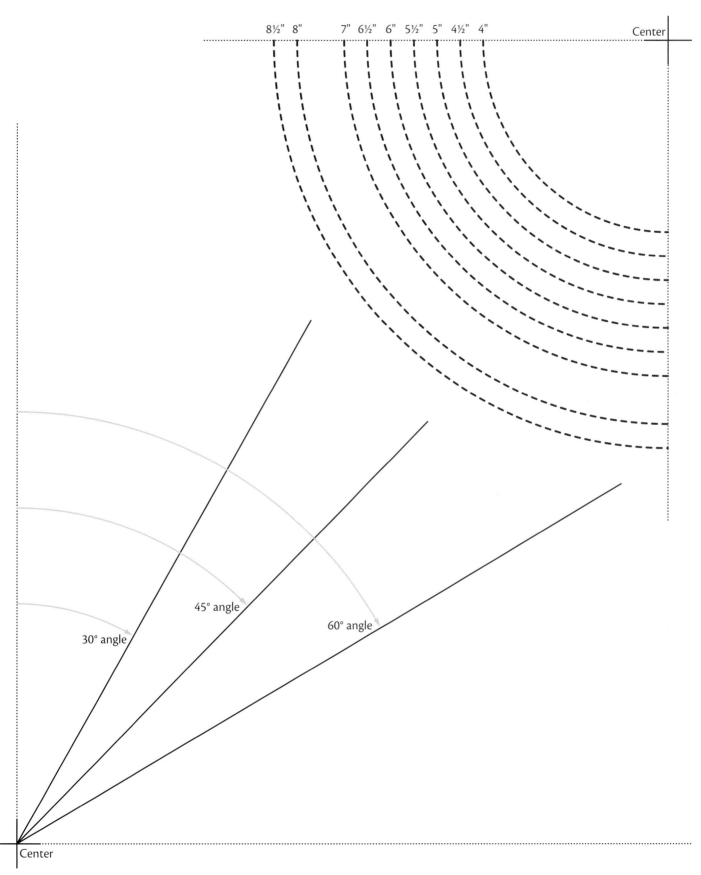

8½" 8"   7" 6½" 6" 5½" 5" 4½" 4"

Center

30° angle

45° angle

60° angle

Center

Size Index

Squares

2"
Comet, 31
Daisy Delight, 80
Floating Clouds and
    Stars, 8
Lucky Clover, 189
Man in the Moon, 9
Pumpkin Vine, 167
Teddy Bear, 10

2½"
Climbing Vine, 99
Daffodil Fancy, 90
Fall Frolic, 11
Fleur-de-Lis, 135
Garden Party, 102
Glorious Morning, 100
Granny Smith's, 107
Heart's Flower, 161
Lattice Blossom, 130
Lazy Leafy, 199
Loveleaf, 193
Pumpkin Vine, 167
Sizzle, 32
Snow Blossom, 95
Snowflake, 176
Spring Promise, 62
Springtime, 75
Star Flower, 75
Wind Swirl, 116

3"
Breezy Blossom, 61
Budding Beauty, 83
Buttercup, 78
Butterfly Dance, 34
Caesar's Heart, 160
Christmas Lights, 174
Country Baskets, 162
Double Feather Wreath, 40
Duck Stroll, 11
Evening Flower, 84
Explorers, 131
Feathers and Flowers, 63
Flower and Beehive, 148
Flower of Youth, 78
Garden Party, 102
Grapevine, 177
Hearts Abloom, 155
Hearts Aflutter, 161
Heart's Flower, 161
Heartsong, 156
Holly, 173

Ivy 2, 181
Petite Fleur, 79
Sheriff's Badge, 26
Shy Violet, 82
Sizzle, 32
Springtime, 75
Stardust, 14
Strawberry Fields, 108
Sunflower, 98
Trailing Vine, 188
Wavelet, 111
Whirlabout, 112
Win Again, 141
Yukon Cable, 115

3½"
Angel, 172
April Love, 150
Autumn Mystery, 188
Baby Birds, 10
Berry Blossom, 105
Between Times, 137
Butterfly Dance, 34
Celestial, 121
Cloverleaf, 195
Daisy Delight, 80
Dandy Daisy, 92
Dog Bone, 36
Evening Flower, 84
Fleur-de-Lis, 135
Floral Spray, 85
Fluttering By, 33
Friendship Blossoms, 65
Grandma's Trellis, 81
Harvest Bloom, 73
Heart Songs, 159
Heart's Flower, 161
Herbal Medley, 106
Hollyberry, 174
Jaunty Jump-Ups, 72
Lemon Twist, 104
Li'l Mitten, 170
Little Star, 32
Loops and Swirls, 124
Loving Hearts, 154
Man in the Moon, 9
Palace Steps, 138
Peach Harvest, 105
Poinsettia Garland, 170
Saw Blade, 128
Shadowbox, 129
Simply Snowflakes, 164
Snow Crystal 1, 175
Spirals and Scrolls, 125

Spring Promise, 62
Star of David, 168
Whirlabout, 112
Woodland Sprig, 185

4"
Angel, 172
Autumn Leaves, 183
Blossom Vine, 89
Bow Tie, 175
Buttercup, 78
Butterfly Garden, 97
Cat Tails, 144
Celebration 1, 59
Climbing Vine, 99
Cloverleaf, 195
Comet, 31
Crown, 26
Dancing Curls, 111
Diamond, 126
Fall Leaf, 187
Fanciful Flowers, 93
Feather Heart, 44
Fish Splash, 118
Floating Lily, 66
Flower and Beehive, 148
Garden Party, 102
Gibraltar, 135
Glorious Morning, 100
Golf Ball, 123
Grandma's Trellis, 81
Grapevine, 177
Guatemala, 123
Hanover, 127
Hearts Abloom, 155
Hearts and Swags, 152
Heavenly Dove, 169
Ivy Leaf, 194
Ivy League, 186
Lattice Blossom, 130
Lilting Leaf, 186
Little Star, 32
Loveleaf, 193
Patch-o'-Pumpkins, 166
Petite Daisy, 92
Piney Woods, 169
Pumpkin Vine, 167
Ravishing Radishes, 104
Rhythm and Bows, 158
Rose Beauty, 76
Shasta Daisy, 74
Shooting Stars, 30
Silver Plume, 38
Sizzle, 32

Snow Blossom, 95
Star in the Window, 129
Starblossom, 140
Sunsprite, 178
Teddy Bear, 10
Today's Touch, 133
Twirl Around, 132
Wandering Summer, 94
Wild Rose, 61
Yukon Cable, 115

4½"
Baby Birds, 10
Bonnie Blue Ribbon, 28
Butterfly Garden, 97
Caesar's Heart, 160
Chinook, 144
Cloverleaf, 195
Comet, 31
Cotton Sprig, 199
Country Baskets, 162
Daisy Delight, 80
Dancing Curls, 111
Dogwood, 94
Fantasia, 139
Floral Delight, 69
Flying Colors, 37
Garden Party, 102
Graceful, 141
Groovy Flowers, 12
Heart Strings, 157
Hearts in Bloom 1, 146
He-Loves-Me, 64
Irish Cable, 142
Ivy League, 186
Just Ducky, 24
Lantern Lily, 60
Lazy Leafy, 199
Leaf Wreath, 185
Leafy Vine, 178
Lida Rose, 60
Lily Bud, 71
Lotus Bud, 67
Loveleaf, 193
Loving Hearts, 154
Magic Vine, 194
Mother's Garden, 182
Oak and Acorn, 166
Paisley, 125
Rippling Waves, 110
Silver Bells, 74
Silver Plume, 38
Snow Blossom, 95
Snow Crystal 1, 175

Snow Crystal 2, 176
Springtime, 75
Star Flower, 75
Swirl, 138
Teddy Bear, 10
Trailing Vine, 188
Twirly Tucks, 137
West Wind, 130
Win Again, 141
Wind Swirl, 116

5"
Belle Fleur, 80
Bow Tie, 175
Breezy Blossom, 61
Budding Vine, 179
Buttercup, 78
Butterfly, 30
Butterfly Dance, 34
Caesar's Heart, 160
Cat Tails, 144
Celtic Chain, 122
Daffodil Fancy, 90
Diamond, 126
Explorers, 131
Fall Frolic, 11
Fish Splash, 118
Fluttering Leaves, 180
Friendship Blossoms, 65
Friendship Vine 1, 190
Glorious Morning, 100
Grandma's Trellis, 81
Granny Smith's, 107
Grapevine, 177
Hanover, 127
Happy Days, 79
Happy Face, 13
Harvest Bloom, 73
Hearts and Flowers, 151
Heart's Flower, 161
Heartsong, 156
Herbal Medley, 106
Ivy 2, 181
Jumping Cat, 25
Just Ducky, 24
Lantern Lily, 60
Lattice Blossom, 130
Leaf Cable, 182
Leaf Spray, 184
Leafy Vine, 178
Lemon Peel, 136
Peace Sign, 13
Petite Fleur, 79
Pinwheel Posey, 69
Poinsettia, 173

Rectangles

If you don't find the dimensions you need, match the height of your rectangle with border motifs and see if repeats fit into your rectangle area.

Triangles
(measured on short side)

3"
Dancing Curls, 111
Dandy Daisy, 92
Lemon Twist, 104
Lilting Leaf, 186

3½"
April Love, 150
Breezy Blossom, 61
Loveleaf, 193

4"
Cloverleaf, 195
Dancing Curls, 111
Floating Lily, 66
Garden Party, 102
Ivy 1, 180
Today's Touch, 133
Wild Rose, 61

4½"
Berry Blossom, 105
Bite o' Melon, 107
Butterfly Dance, 34
Double Feather Wreath, 40
Heart Songs, 159
Lilting Leaf, 186
Lotus Bud, 67
Star in the Window, 129

5"
Between Times, 137
Blossom Vine, 89
Bow Tie, 175
Caesar's Heart, 160
Celestial, 121
Glorious Morning, 100
He-Loves-Me, 64
Pumpkin Vine, 167
Star Flower, 75

5½"
Autumn Leaves, 183
Caesar's Heart, 160
Poinsettia Garland, 170
Pyramids of the Sun, 140
Sunshine, 8

6"
Desert Sunset, 24
Double Feather Wreath, 40
Evening Flower, 84
Grapevine, 177
Harvest Bloom, 73
Holly Wreath, 171
Lily Bud, 71
Oak and Acorn, 166

Petite Fleur, 79
Spring Delight, 162
Strawberry Fields, 108
Today's Touch, 133
Twinkling Stars, 23

6½"
April Love, 150
Bamboo, 183
Hearts in Bloom 1, 146
Hearts in Bloom 2, 147
Ivy 2, 181
Lida Rose, 60
Ritzy, 134
Tulip Wreath, 95

7"
Cocheco, 39
Country Baskets, 162
Daisy Field, 67
Fizz Hearts, 33
Shy Violet, 82
Spring Leaves, 192
Tea Leaf, 184

7½"
Grandma's Trellis, 81
Man in the Moon, 9
Pyramids of the Sun, 140

8"
First Bloom, 63
Fizz Leaves, 189
Floral Medley, 87
Holly, 173
Rippling Waves, 110

8½"
Candle Flame, 113
Feather Wreath 2, 48
Hearts Around, 159
Rhythm and Bows, 158
Sheriff's Badge, 26

9"
Bamboo, 183
Celebration 2, 114
Fancy Feathers, 41
Rainbow Sherbet, 9

9½"
Sheriff's Badge, 26
Tropical Fling, 70

10"
Daffodil Fancy, 90
Kaleidoscope, 50
Lazy Leafy, 199

10½"
Hearts in Bloom 2, 147
Persian Rose, 68

11"
Dandy Daisy, 92
Friendship Vine 1, 190
Loops and Swirls, 124
Poinsettia, 173

12"
Feather Wreath 2, 48
Sparkling Flower, 77

13"
Tropical Fling, 70

14"
Limerick Waves, 55

15"
Poinsettia, 173

Borders
A motif that fits in a square can also be used for a border. Select one with the same measurement as the border width you wish to fill and repeat the design along the lengths.

1"
Floral Medley, 87

1½"
Ivy 1, 180
Leaf Cable, 182

2"
Amish Traditions, 155
Arrowhead, 120
Cloverleaf, 195
Comet, 31
Daisy Delight, 80
Dandy Daisy, 92
Feathers and Flowers, 63
Floral Medley, 87
Heart Strings, 157
Hearts Aflutter, 161
He-Loves-Me, 64
Jaunty Jump-Ups, 72
Leaf Spray, 184
Petite Daisy, 92
Silver Plume, 38
Snow Blossom, 95
Spring Promise, 62
Summer Leaves, 190
Teddy Bear, 10

2½"
April Love, 150
Bonnie Blue Ribbon, 28
Bows and Bells, 163
Butterfly Garden, 97

Cloverleaf, 195
Continuous Cable, 143
Double Feather Wreath, 40
Fleur-de-Lis, 135
Fluttering Leaves, 180
High Seas, 132
Lattice Blossom, 130
Lemon Peel, 136
Lilting Leaf, 186
Snow Crystal 2, 176
Spring Promise, 62
Springtime, 75
Trailing Vine, 188
Twirl Around, 132
Wild Rose, 61
Wind Swirl, 116
Yukon Cable, 115

3"
Berry Blossom, 105
Between Times, 137
Bows and Borders, 136
Breezy Blossom, 61
Budding Beauty, 83
Buttercup, 78
Catch of the Day, 103
Celebration 1, 59
Cloverleaf, 195
Dandy Daisy, 92
Desert Sunset, 24
Diamond, 126
Flower of Youth, 78
Friendship Blossoms, 65
Friendship Vine 2, 191
Golf Ball, 123
Granny Smith's, 107
Grapevine, 177
Heart Songs, 159
Hearts Abloom, 155
Hearts Aflutter, 161
Heart's Flower, 161
Heartsong, 156
He-Loves-Me, 64
High Seas, 132
Holly Wreath, 171
Hollyberry, 174
Ivy 1, 180
Lemon Twist, 104
Lilac Leaf, 200
Lotus Bud, 67
Loveleaf, 193
Pumpkin Vine, 167
Ribbon Reel, 113
Shadowbox, 129
Sizzle, 32
Spring Delight, 162
Springtime, 75
Starblossom, 140

Cloverleaf, 195
Continuous Cable, 143
Double Feather Wreath, 40
Fleur-de-Lis, 135
Fluttering Leaves, 180
High Seas, 132
Lattice Blossom, 130
Lemon Peel, 136
Lilting Leaf, 186
Snow Crystal 2, 176
Spring Promise, 62
Springtime, 75
Trailing Vine, 188
Twirl Around, 132
Wild Rose, 61
Wind Swirl, 116
Yukon Cable, 115

Stardust, 14
Strawberry Fields, 108
Today's Touch, 133
Trellis Vine, 196
Tulip Wreath, 95
Wavelet, 111
Whirlabout, 112
Wild Rose, 61
Win Again, 141
Yukon Cable, 115

3½"
Arrowhead, 120
Autumn Breeze, 114
Autumn Leaves, 183
Autumn Mystery, 188
Baby Birds, 10
Berry Blossom, 105
Between Times, 137
Bite o' Melon, 107
Budding Vine, 179
Butterfly Dance, 34
Cable Border, 128
Caesar's Heart, 160
Cat Tails, 144
Celestial, 121
Cloverleaf, 195
Comet, 31
Dandy Daisy, 92
Diamond, 126
Dog Bone, 36
Fancy Feathers, 41
Feathers and Flowers, 63
Fish Splash, 118
Fleur-de-Lis, 135
Floating Lily, 66
Fluttering By, 33
Flying Colors, 37
Glorious Morning, 100
Grandma's Trellis, 81
Heart Songs, 159
Heart Strings, 157
Hearts Around, 159
Heart's Flower, 161
Hearts in Bloom 1, 146
He-Loves-Me, 64
Herbal Medley, 106
Holly, 173
Jumping Cat, 25
Leaf Spray, 184
Leafy Bough, 198
Li'l Mitten, 170
Little Star, 32
Lucky Clover, 189
Man in the Moon, 9
Oak and Acorn, 166
Palace Steps, 138
Peach Harvest, 105

Alphabetical Index